Health Matters!

Volume 2
Mental Health: Depression, Suicide, and Other Issues

General Editor

William M. Kane, Ph.D.
University of New Mexico

Advisors

Marilee Foglesong
Former Young Adult Coordinator
New York Public Library

James Robinson III, Ed.D.
Texas A&M University

Stephen Stewart, DrPH
James Madison University

GROLIER

Old Sherman Turnpike
Danbury, Connecticut 06816

Published 2002 by Grolier Educational
Old Sherman Turnpike
Danbury, CT 06816

Developed, Designed, and Produced by BOOK BUILDERS LLC

For information address the publisher:
Grolier Educational, Old Sherman Turnpike, Danbury, CT 06816

Photo Credits
The following photographs are used by permission and through the courtesy
of CMSP: 6 (Potter), 34, 42 (Peter Berndt Md), 55 (T. McCarthy),
59, 71 (E. Nelson),78 (Sean O'Brien), 83 (Smith), 86 (SPL), 89 (Mark).

*Every endeavor has been made to obtain permission to use copyrighted material.
The publishers would appreciate errors or omissions being brought to their attention.*

Library of Congress Cataloging-in-Publication Data

Health matters!
        p. cm.
        Contents: v. 1. Addiction: tobacco, alcohol, and other drugs—v. 2. Mental health
depression, suicide, and other issues—v. 3. Sexuality and pregnancy—v. 4. Physical
activity, weight, and eating disorders—v. 5. Injuries and violence—v. 6. Environmental
poisoning—v. 7. HIV infections, AIDS, and STDs—v. 8. Diseases and disabling conditions.
        ISBN 0-7172-5575-1 (set: alk. paper)—ISBN 0-7172-5576-X (v. 1: alk. paper)—
ISBN 0-7172-5577-8 (v. 2: alk. paper)—ISBN 0-7172-5578-6 (v. 3: alk. paper)—
ISBN 0-7172-5579-4 (v. 4: alk. paper)—ISBN 0-7172-5580-8 (v. 5: alk. paper)—
ISBN 0-7172-5581-6 (v. 6: alk. paper)—ISBN 0-7172-5582-4 (v. 7: alk. paper)—
ISBN 0-7172-5583-2 (v. 8: alk. paper)
        1. Health—Juvenile literature. 2. Health behavior—Juvenile literature. [1. Health.] I.
Grolier Educational (Firm)

RA777 H386 2002
613—dc21

                                                                    2001040248

Contents

What is the greatest threat to my health? If I begin smoking, will I be able to quit? Am I at risk of acquiring HIV infection and AIDS? How dangerous is it to ride in a car with a driver who has been drinking? Do I need to take vitamins to be healthy? How much sun does it take to cause skin cancer? Will crack cocaine hurt me if I just try it one time?

Such questions are typical of what people ask themselves regarding their health. We are constantly faced with making decisions that will affect our health and safety. This eight-volume reference set, *Health Matters!*, provides answers to myriad health-related questions by offering accurate and straightforward information on health topics ranging from addiction to environmental poisoning to infectious and chronic diseases. These volumes are also a valuable tool for conducting research, writing papers, and getting answers to personal questions about health and your body.

Over the past 30 years, in my capacity as a public school teacher and university professor, I have had the opportunity to work with teenagers, teachers, and librarians. As a head of national health and medical organizations I have also worked with surgeon generals, U.S. secretaries for health, and congressional leaders to help improve the health of all Americans.

As general editor of this encyclopedia I have drawn not only on these experiences but also on my experience as a member of the writing team that developed the *National Health Education Standards*—guidelines that define what students need to know and do to become health literate. Additionally, my contribution to these volumes reflects more than 30 years' participation in the development of the federal government's *Healthy People* initiatives outlined most recently in *Healthy People 2010*, a framework of national health objectives published by the U.S. Department of Health and Human Services.

Health Matters! blends the science and practice of disease prevention and health promotion with the daily concerns and decisions facing American teenagers and adults of all ages. I hope these volumes will answer your questions about health-related matters and arm you with the knowledge you need to make lifelong healthy decisions.

William M. Kane
General Editor

How to Use This Book

Health Matters! contains up-to-date information about the many topics and issues related to health and wellness—including addiction; mental health; sexuality and pregnancy; physical activity, weight and eating disorders; injuries and violence; environment poisoning; HIV infection, AIDS, and sexually transmitted diseases; and diseases and disabling conditions. The content in the set addresses all the issues and topics contained in the *National Health Education Standards* for achieving health literacy.

The set is divided into eight volumes, each focusing on a specific health-related topic. Within each volume the information is organized into six different sections. "Healthy Living: Teen Choices and Actions" prompts readers to consider the effect that their actions can have on their future health and life. "Who Me? Check It Out!" offers short quizzes that readers can use to assess how their current behaviors may affect their health. The heart of each volume, "Just the Facts," is an alphabetical encyclopedia of entries that provide in-depth facts and information young researchers need. "Concerns and Fears" looks at various issues that are of particular concern to teens. In "It Can't Happen to Me" readers will find stories about teenagers who have faced difficult health problems and struggled to overcome them. The final section, "Straight Talk," provides honest answers to some of the hard questions about health issues that students typically ask of adults.

Darrell Kozlowski and Charles Roebuck
Editors

Healthy Living: Teen Choices and Actions

Remember when everyone used to ask you, What do you want to be when you grow up? Maybe they should have asked, What do you want to be *if you decide* to grow up? With almost every action you take today you choose not only who you will be today, tomorrow, and in five or ten years but also whether you will even be at all.

First, the bad news: The best choices for you can be the hardest to make, and some of the teenagers you know today may find their lives have changed forever due to poor decisions they have made because of mental illness or emotional problems. Instead of having a happy, fulfilling life, they may have lives filled with unhappiness, disappointment, and even downright misery. Some may even die before they reach age 25, perhaps because they chose to take their own life rather than deal with the challenges that life brings.

The good news? You have the power to shape your life (to some extent) and ensure a happy and fulfilling life. You can choose to confront your problems and learn to deal with them, and you can take steps to combat DEPRESSION or other emotional or mental problems. In fact, you may have already made choices that will help ensure good MENTAL HEALTH and affect the person you will be at age 25. And good mental health habits will pay off as you get older.

But I'm young, you say. And right now you feel pretty good most of the time, and you have plenty of energy. It may be hard to imagine any of this changing. Why think about it now? Look around. You may know kids who are angry, depressed, or under a lot of STRESS; who suffer from severe ANXIETY, or who take lots of risks.

Of the approximately 30,500 Americans who die of suicide each year, almost 25 percent are young people between the ages of 15 and 24. According to the CENTERS FOR DISEASE CONTROL AND PREVENTION (CDC), teens attempt suicide more than any other age group. Suicide is the third leading cause of death among teens. In *Mental Health: A Report of the Surgeon General,* published in 2001, between 10 and 15 percent of teens were reported to have *some* symptoms of depression. Five percent of teens from ages 9 to 17 in the United States suffer from serious depression.

That may make the choices for the next five or ten years seem pretty easy. Assuming you are basically healthy, all you have to do is avoid risky activities and not kill yourself. Right? But what about the less obvious choices, decisions that make you who you are–and who you will be in ten years–choices like who your friends are, how long you stay in school, what you do for fun?

Imagine describing yourself this way at 25: "I work part-time in a supermarket and spend the rest of the time hanging out with friends playing video games and drinking beer or doing drugs when I can afford them. I feel anxious a lot and can be pretty moody. I still live at home, even though I don't get along that well with my parents, because my paycheck is too small to cover the rent on even a small apartment. I don't think about the future very much because it just depresses me. I sometimes feel like a failure and wonder whether my life will ever amount to anything."

Consider this alternative: "I love my job; I'm the senior manager of an upscale clothing store, and there is plenty of room for advancement with the company. I recently moved into my own condo in a really nice neighborhood. I'm happily involved in a serious relationship—we've been dating steadily for two years and are talking about marriage in the very near future. Despite my busy life, I still find time to spend with my parents, brothers and sisters, and friends. I feel very positive and confident about my life right now." Because you're quite modest, you fail to mention that you've been putting money aside for future retirement and have made a good start on achieving financial security.

Okay, both scenarios are extremes. The point is, the choices you make *right now,* every day, are heading you in one direction or the other.

SAFE BEHAVIORS ARE SMART CHOICES

You can probably make some good guesses about which behaviors–ways you choose to act based on your own values–will keep you headed in the direction you want to go. (You also can choose your actions, which are the specific things you do that make up your patterns of behavior.) The tough part is making the smart choices about behavior, then acting on them.

According to the Joint Committee on National Health Education Standards, which define what kids ought to know and be able to do, the first safe behavior is making smart choices when it comes to your body and mind, choices based on solid, reliable information. The other safe behaviors, in a nutshell, are exercising, eating right, reducing stress, and getting medical help when you need it.

Making the best choices for your own body and mind is mainly about being informed and thinking things through. Say that you're feeling very tired and unhappy lately. You haven't been sleeping or eating well, and you are having trouble concentrating in school and feel that your life is worthless. Your friends are concerned about you; one friend gives you a book about depression. You read that depression is a serious problem among teens—one that can be treated successfully. Your friends are very supportive and encourage you to seek professional help. You do, and soon your life and outlook begin to improve.

How about exercise? Here's a news flash: Dancing once a week for three hours, playing a game of football or basketball a few times a week, or biking ten minutes to school is not enough. The secret to feeling as good in ten years as you do right now is *vigorous activity that lasts at least 20 minutes at a time at least three times a week* (for instance, fast walking, jogging, biking, or swimming). *Plus* regular exercise *every day,* such as participation in physical education, games, or sports.

Exercise is just as important as eating right. Making smart choices about food might seem simple, but lots of people find it difficult. First, the simple part: Eat lots of fruits and vegetables, cut down on fried, fatty (red meat, cheese), and sugar-rich foods, and get informed about good nutrition (everything to do with how you eat and how your body uses food). Here are two examples of eating choices some would find hard: Grab a few donuts for breakfast every day, or sit down and have cereal and juice? You no doubt know what the *best* choice is, but how often will you make that choice? Given the choice of chocolate cake or a baked apple for dessert, how often will you choose the baked apple? (Check out "Healthy Eating Tips" at www.cdc.gov/nccd-php/dnpa/heal_eat.htm. The Centers for Disease Control and Prevention website is a great resource for all kinds of information on health and disease.)

Starting to feel stressed from thinking about all these choices? Fine. Stress is natural (it's a physical, chemical, or emotional factor that causes tension in the mind or body). Stress can come from positive *and* negative events in life—such as arguments, changing schools, moving, a big date, falling in love, the death of a pet or a person, feeling left out, or winning a prize. You can probably guess the best way to cope with stress—relax. The least stressed people spend time every week—or every day—doing whatever it is that they find relaxing.

The last area of safe behavior calls for arranging a visit to the doctor, therapist, or another health professional when you suspect something is wrong with you. Say you have an oddly shaped mole that you're afraid is skin cancer. Perhaps you've been having weird thoughts or feelings and are worried that you're mentally ill. Or maybe you have genital itching, and you feel both embarrassed and worried that it might be from an STD. (A sexually transmitted disease is an infection passed from person to person by intimate sexual contact.) If your condition is a serious one, the smart choice is to find out its cause—*now*. Medical tests can detect many diseases and problems early. Serious diseases like diabetes, heart disease, HIV, and many kinds of cancer can be fought more effectively if treatment starts early. Likewise, mental and emotional problems benefit from early diagnosis and treatment.

RISKY BEHAVIORS AND ACTIONS

You knew this section was coming, right? If there are safe behaviors and smart choices likely to keep you alive and well for the next decade, there are also unsafe ones. And there is a fact that intelligent people like to ignore: A person can be very smart and still make dumb choices, including choosing to practice risky behaviors.

The U.S. Centers for Disease Control and Prevention (CDC) (the main federal agency charged with protecting health and safety) lists **six risky behavior categories.**

Poor Diet. Here is what can lie ahead for people with consistently poor eating habits—people who are careless about what food they eat or who eat too much or too little. Eating certain foods—raw eggs, for instance (say, in uncooked cookie dough)—raises your chances of getting sick from the bacteria or other toxic agents in those foods. There are more than 250 diseases that food carries. Food-borne illnesses include cholera, salmonella, typhoid fever, and gastroenteritis (severe diarrhea and vomiting). Related outcomes, besides death, include spontaneous abortion and blood poisoning.

Lack of Exercise. Obesity (usually weighing 20 percent or more of the expected weight for a given height) affects almost every area of life, from ordinary activity to sports, from self-confidence to energy levels to the kinds of clothes we can buy. Overweight people are at greater risk for stroke, heart disease, or osteoporosis. During a stroke an artery in the brain ruptures or gets clogged, causing paralysis (not being able to move) or death. Osteoporosis is a progressive loss of bone mass, which increases the risk of bone breakage, usually for older people. *But beginning in childhood,* people who get too little calcium put themselves at serious risk for the disease.

Eating disorders like anorexia and bulimia can be even more dangerous than simple overeating. Of forty teenagers you know, one probably eats far too little (anorexia) or binges on food and then purges by vomiting or taking laxatives (bulimia). Anorexia can damage a person's heart, liver, and kidneys. The vomiting of bulimia often causes constant stomach pain,

Six Risky Behavior Catagories
Poor diet
Lack of exercise
Smoking
Actions that lead to unintentional and intentional injuries
Alcohol or drug abuse
Sexual practices that increase the risk of STDs, HIV infection, and unintended pregnancy

damage to the stomach and kidneys, and tooth decay. Both anorexia and bulimia can be fatal.

While people with bulimia often exercise too much, what about people who get too little exercise? They risk harm from all the conditions associated with poor diet and obesity, and also from high blood pressure, non-insulin-dependent diabetes, cancers, high cholesterol, back pain, feelings of stress, anxiety, and depression.

Smoking. For every teenager, smoking is almost guaranteed to have bad short-term health effects—damage to the respiratory system, addiction to nicotine, and some risk of other drug use. Statistics from the American Cancer Society and the CDC show that if you smoke regularly now, as a teenager, you will probably smoke throughout adulthood. *Then* you can count on *long-term* health consequences. Compared to nonsmokers, smokers are more likely to:
- Die seven years younger
- Die from lung cancer (if you are male, 22 times more likely; if you are female, 12 times more likely)
- Die from bronchitis and emphysema (males and females are at ten times the risk)
- Die from cardiovascular disease, such as heart attack or strokes, (both males and females are at three times the risk)

Unintentional and Intentional Injuries. Few people are injured and killed as a result of accidents, which are random events that cannot be prevented. Most victims of unintentional injuries, which are almost always the direct result of actions that can be avoided, such as drinking and driving. Intentional injuries, which result from acts of violence, can also be prevent by identifying potentially dangerous situations ahead of time and taking action to avoid those risks.

Alcohol or Drug Abuse. There is no good news about drinking alcohol or using illegal drugs. And the earlier kids start drinking, the more likely they will be to develop a problem with alcohol or drugs later in life (look at www.kidshealth.org/teen for good information on all health issues). Teens who drink are more likely to be sexually active and to have unsafe, unprotected sex. When they drink, they may find it harder to resist unwanted sexual advances, and they are more vulnerable to sexual assault. Resulting pregnancies and STDs can change—or even end—lives.

The most widely used illegal drug in the United States is marijuana, which is often called a gateway drug because frequent smoking can lead to the use of stronger drugs. Marijuana is as tough on your lungs as cigarettes—steady smokers often suffer coughs, wheezing, and frequent colds. Of all abused substances, inhalants are the most likely to cause severe toxic reaction and death. Inhalants include glues, paint thinners, dry-cleaning fluids, gasoline, felt-tip marker fluid, correction fluid, hair spray, and spray paint. *Using inhalants, even one time, can kill you.*

Risky Sexual Practices. Equally harmful are HIV/AIDs and other infectious diseases. About one in four people between the ages of 15 and 55 will get an STD. Some can lead to long-term problems such as infertility (the inability to have a baby or father one) or even death if they are left untreated. STDs include chlamydia, genital herpes, genital warts, gonorrhea, hepatitis, HIV/AIDS, pubic lice (crabs), and syphilis.

Today, most adolescents infected with HIV are exposed to the virus through sexual intercourse or injection drug use, according to NIAID (National Institute of Allergy and Infectious Diseases). HIV, which causes AIDS, is the sixth leading cause of death for U.S. young people 15 to 24 years of age. *Most young adults with AIDS were likely infected with HIV as adolescents*, because the average period of time from HIV infection to the development of AIDS is ten years. Almost 18 percent of all reported cases of AIDS in the United States have occurred in people between the ages of 20 and 29.

WHAT'S TO COME

The rest of this book is packed with almost everything you ever wanted to know about mental health, depression, and suicide. In the next section, "Who Me? Check It Out!" you will find tools to assess your own risk-taking behaviors. In "Just the Facts" are definitions of these topics, from ABUSE AND MENTAL HEALTH to VIOLENCE AND MENTAL HEALTH, followed by a section that addresses your "Concerns and Fears." The section called "It Can't Happen to Me" includes stories of teenagers to whom some of these bad things and problems *did* happen. And in the final section, "Straight Talk," you will find honest answers to some of the hard questions about mental or emotional health problems, depression, and suicide.

Special feature boxes provide health updates, help readers determine fact from folklore, focus on health-related behaviors in which teens are at special risk, and explore sensitive topics about which experts disagree or teens often lack understanding. The back of each volume contains a comprehensive glossary that gathers and defines keywords from all volumes; a list for further reading and Internet sites that suggests opportunities for additional research; and a directory of health-related services, organizations, help sites, and hotlines . Finally, a set index will help the reader locate topics and terms through all eight volumes.

Health Matters! also provides a number of helpful reference features. Difficult words are printed in boldface type and defined in margin boxes as keywords. Cross-references that appear in small capital letters refer the reader to another entry in the same volume. Cross-references that appear in boldface and in small capital letters define the word as a keyword and also refer the reader to another entry in the same volume. Boldfaced and italicized cross-references, followed by a volume and number, lead the reader to related information that appears in another volume in the set. At the end of many entries "see also" cross-references point the reader to entries with related information in the same volume. Finally, some entries may also be followed by "More Sources," listing web sites that contain information related to the topic of the entry.

Who Me? Check It Out!

For many people the hard part about examining their risky behaviors is that once they have really looked at them, it is even harder to deny that they are choosing to behave in ways that are dangerous to their mental health and happiness—and maybe even life itself.

The choices are not always simple: If I have a problem, should I ignore it, or should I figure out what's going wrong? When my life is stressful, is it okay to take drugs so I can relax or "get away"? Which is more important, avoiding embarrassment by not talking about "private" things or getting good advice from an adult or counselor? Would it be worse to hurt someone's feelings by telling them about things they do that bother me or to go on feeling bad about myself? All of the behaviors in the following reality checks are things you control. No one can do the reality checks for you, and no one needs to know your answers. You are the only person who knows what you are really doing, thinking, and feeling. And naturally, you are also the person in charge of making positive changes if you decide you need to.

Read each of the following questions and determine the answer that best describes you or your behavior. Keep track of your answers on a separate sheet of paper.

REALITY CHECK 1

What Are My Chances of Developing Mental Health Problems or Mental Illness?

1. Do any of your close biological relatives (parents, grandparents, siblings) have a mental illness?

   Yes   No   Not sure

2. Were you abused as a young child, or did you ever experience an extremely frightening event, such as a near-fatal car crash or shooting?

   Yes   No   Not sure

3. How many prescription medications do you take on a regular basis?

   0   1 to 3   4 or more

4. In the past 30 days how many times have you used alcohol or a drug such as marijuana or cocaine?

   0   1 to 3   4 or more

5. On a scale of 0 to 5, where 0 is "no stress" and 5 is "very high stress," what level of stress do you experience most of the time?

   0   1 to 3   4 or more

6. How many times have you been in serious trouble at school or with the law?

   0   1 to 3   4 or more

7. Which approach to a troubling problem are you more likely to take?

   A. Ignore it and hope it will go away
   B. Solve it and get on with your life

Check Yourself

If you answered "yes" to . . .

Question 1: You may be at higher-than-average risk of developing the same or a similar mental illness as your relative.

Question 2: You may have an increased risk of developing certain mental health problems, such as anxiety, or specific mental illnesses, such as phobias.

If you answered "4 or more" to . . .

Question 3: You may have an increased chance of developing symptoms of a mental illness such as an anxiety disorder.

Question 4: You may be abusing alcohol or another substance, and this can be both a symptom and a cause of a mental health problem or mental illness.

Question 5: You may be increasing your risk of developing various mental illnesses, from anxiety disorders to schizophrenia.

Question 6: You may have emotional problems or a personality disorder, which is a type of mental illness.

If you answered "A" to . . .

Question 7: You may be relying on unhealthy ways of coping with problems that could worsen any mental health problem or mental illness you already have.

Debriefing Reality Check 1

This self-check is not about whether a behavior is right or wrong or good or bad. It is about realistically assessing your risk of mental illness and whether certain behaviors or situations may increase that *risk.*

Question 1: Most mental illnesses run in families and probably have a genetic component. Just as your genes can increase your chances of developing heart disease or cancer, they can also make you more or less likely to develop bipolar disorder, schizophrenia, and other mental illnesses. Therefore, if you have a close biological relative with a mental illness, you may have a greater-than-average chance of developing it as well.

Question 2: Extremely abusive situations and frightening events, especially when they create feelings of helplessness or terror, can scar people for life. Children are especially vulnerable to these effects because they do not have the maturity or experience to deal with them. Children may appear to be okay on the outside while suffering on the inside, or they may develop lifelong personality problems, such as excessive shyness or low self-esteem. Some people develop mental illnesses, such as posttraumatic stress disorder, because of such experiences.

Question 3: Many of the medications that are commonly prescribed for medical problems can cause symptoms of mental illness. For example, the drug Valium, which is widely used to treat anxiety, can cause memory loss, a symptom of a number of mental illnesses, including dissociative amnesia. Several prescription medications used to treat asthma or high blood pressure can cause symptoms of anxiety disorders, and decongestants can cause panic attacks.

Question 4: Abuse of substances such as alcohol or other drugs can cause mental health problems, such as memory loss and hallucinations. It can contribute to the development of such mental illnesses as bipolar disorder and anxiety disorders. Substance abuse can also lead to trouble in school and with the law and to reckless behavior, such as drunk driving and unprotected sex.

Question 5: High levels of stress can cause or worsen many mental illnesses, including adjustment disorder, anxiety disorders, schizophrenia, and bipolar disorder.

Question 6: Frequent run-ins with authority may be a sign of acting out, or behaving recklessly in order to avoid thinking about a stressful situation or painful emotion. Acting out is an unhealthy behavior that some people exhibit when trying to cope with emotional problems, but it usually makes problems worse instead of better. Frequent trouble with authority may also be a sign of antisocial personality disorder, which is a serious mental illness.

Question 7: Avoiding or ignoring problems or trying to forget about painful situations and emotions are unhealthy ways of coping that are generally referred to as *defense mechanisms*. They are unhealthy because they do not eliminate the problems, which are therefore likely to continue to cause emotional turmoil and pain. Reliance on defense mechanisms can worsen mental health problems and mental illnesses.

Read the following questions and determine the answer that best describes your behavior. Keep track of your answers on a separate sheet of paper.

REALITY CHECK 2

What Are My Chances of Developing Depression?

1. Do any of your close biological relatives (parents, grandparents, siblings) have a mood disorder, such as depression or bipolar disorder?

   Yes   No   Not sure

2. Do you have a serious physical illness or disability that limits your activities or that can be life-threatening?

   Yes   No   Not sure

3. Have you ever suffered from depression in the past?

   Yes   No   Not sure

4. Have you experienced a major loss within the past few months, such as the death of a close relative or the breakup of a serious romantic relationship?

   Yes   No

5. Do you ever drink alcohol or use drugs to "drown your sorrows" or try to feel better?

   Yes   No

6. How often do you feel down on yourself or dislike yourself?

   Never   Sometimes   Usually

7. Which approach to a case of "the blues" are you more likely to take?

   A. Stay in your room until you feel better
   B. Go out with friends to cheer up

Check Yourself

If you answered "yes" to . . .

Question 1 or 2: Your family history may put you at higher-than-average risk of developing depression.

Question 3: You may have an increased risk of becoming depressed again.

Question 4: Because of recent events in your life, your risk of developing depression is greater than usual at this time.

Question 5: If you are not already depressed, substance abuse may increase your risk of developing depression.

If you answered "usually" to . . .

Question 6: You could have or maybe at risk for developing low self-esteem, which may increase your risk of depression.

If you answered "A" to . . .

Question 7: You may be increasing the risk that your case of "the blues" will develop into more serious depression. You maybe relying on unhealthy ways of coping with your problems, perhaps making them worse.

Debriefing Reality Check 2

This self-check is not about whether a behavior is right or wrong or good or bad. It is about realistically assessing your risk of developing depression and whether certain behaviors or situations may increase that *risk*.

Question 1: Depression and other mood disorders appear to run in families, so a tendency to develop them is probably inherited. Therefore, having a close biological relative with depression usually increases a person's risk of developing the disorder.

Question 2: Suffering from a serious physical illness, such as cancer or AIDS, makes many people more likely to develop depression. Pain and suffering, limitations on normal everyday activities, side effects of medications, money worries, and fear of dying may all contribute to the risk.

Question 3: Having experienced an episode of depression in the past increases the risk of having another episode. And the more episodes of depression that one has already experienced, the greater the risk that future episodes will occur.

Question 4: Suffering a major loss may trigger the development of depression, especially in someone who is already at increased risk because of a family history of the disease. Depression stemming from a personal loss may occur at any age.

Question 5: Alcohol, which is the most widely abused substance, often makes people feel depressed while they are intoxicated. Many people believe that alcohol is a stimulant that helps them "loosen up," but it is really a depressant. Cocaine and similar stimulant drugs tend to cause feelings of depression after the "high" of the drugs has worn off. Often the depression is worse.

Question 6. People with low self-esteem usually lack self-confidence and a sense of control over their own lives. Such feelings may increase the risk of depression. Often times the feeling of low self-esteem begin at an early age and grow as a person enters the teen years, thus increasing the risk for developing depression.

Question 7. Getting involved with other people rather than brooding alone when you are feeling down is one of the best ways to prevent depression from developing. Being socially active can also help people bounce back from an episode of depression. People who develop positive relationships and who have family and friends they can rely on are less likely to develop depression. A strong support group often helps people get over the "blues" before depression develops.

Just the Facts: Mental Health— Depression, Suicide, and Other Issues A-Z

The first step in effectively dealing with a mental health problem is to understand it—to know enough about it to take appropriate action and to prevent it from happening again if at all possible. Reliable mental health information can also give you a sense of control over the situation and ease unwarranted fears. Without this information you are at the mercy of unknown, perhaps scary, mental processes. You can only wait to see what happens.

This section provides you with knowledge that will help you take charge of your own mental and emotional health. It contains accurate and honest information about dozens of chronic mental illnesses, life-threatening behaviors, emotional conditions, and medical treatments. It tells why specific mental health or emotional problems occur, who is most likely to get them, what their signs and symptoms are, what happens when they are treated properly, how to prevent them from happening to you, and how they can be cured or treated. In short, this section contains something that is often difficult for teens to find—up-to-date and useful facts based on the best scientific and medical information available.

ABUSE AND MENTAL HEALTH Abuse is mistreating or intentionally injuring another person. It often leads to mental health problems. Abuse typically occurs within the family. Women and children are the most common targets of abuse. Elderly family members are often abused as well.

Victims of abuse are likely to experience feelings of rejection, worthlessness, helplessness, and emotional pain. Not surprisingly, they have a greater chance of developing a MENTAL ILLNESS such as DEPRESSION. In cases of severe abuse in childhood victims may develop a very serious DISSOCIATIVE DISORDER called dissociative identity disorder.

Types of Abuse. Abuse can be physical, emotional, or sexual. Physical abuse includes spanking, pushing, shaking, punching, and burning. Emotional abuse can range from repeated name calling to constant criticism. Sexual abuse includes any type of unwanted touching or sexual attention, as well as sexual assault. All three types of abuse can cause emotional pain and damage MENTAL HEALTH.

Epidemiology. Abuse is a major public health issue. Each year in the United States alone almost 2 million children are abused. More than a thousand children die each year because of abuse. Most of them are under five years of age, and half are under one year of age.

People inflict abuse when they cannot control their impulses. They are more likely to be abusive if they have certain PERSONALITY DISORDERS or if they abuse alcohol or other substances. People are also more likely to be abusive if they are under too much STRESS. Stress can result from a crisis, such as loss of a job, or from day-to-day concerns, such as caring for a terminally ill relative. Stress is more likely to lead to abusive behavior in people with inadequate SOCIAL SUPPORT SYSTEMS and poor coping skills.

Signs of Abuse. Victims of abuse, particularly children and teens, may be afraid to report the abuse. As a result, family members, doctors, teachers, and other professionals involved with children should be aware of the signs and symptoms of abuse. They include multiple bruises, unexplained injuries, sudden changes in behavior, loss of appetite, and problems in school. For example, a teenage boy who has pent-up anger from abuse at home may turn his anger against his peers and become the class bully.

Reporting Abuse. Health professionals, teachers, and child-care workers are required by law to report cases of suspected child abuse to a child welfare or health and human services agency. Individual citizens are not required to report abuse, but they are encouraged to make it known if they suspect it. If you are being abused or know someone who is, tell a doctor, teacher, minister, or other trusted adult.

Treatment. Some victims of abuse may need PSYCHOTHERAPY or DRUG THERAPY to cope with low self-esteem, depression, or other mental health problems associated with the abuse. Shelters, crisis centers, and hotlines are available to abuse victims who need help escaping from an abusive situation.

MORE SOURCES See www.ama.org

ADDICTION AND MENTAL HEALTH An overwhelming need to use a substance, such as alcohol or other drug, or to engage in a behavior, such as gambling or stealing, despite its harmful effects. *Addiction* (see Volume 1) can cause ANXIETY and other MENTAL HEALTH PROBLEMS. Conversely, some MENTAL ILLNESSES, such as DEPRESSION and SCHIZOPHRENIA, can increase the risk of addiction.

Types of Addiction. Addiction can be physical, psychological, or both. *Physical addiction* can occur with alcohol or other substances. In physical addiction there is a biological need for the substance, and symptoms such as headaches or trembling develop when it is withdrawn. *Psychological addiction* can occur with behaviors as well as substances. In psychological addiction there is a psychological need for the "high" that the substance or behavior produces.

Risk Factors for Addiction. Risk of addiction is greater if a close biological relative has an addiction, because the condition tends to run in families. The risk is also greater if friends use addictive substances. In addition, depression and STRESS can increase the chances of addiction, as can low self-esteem and poor coping skills.

Effects of Addiction. Long-term use of addictive substances can do great harm to the body. For example, alcohol can cause cirrhosis, a potentially fatal liver disease, inhalants can lead to seizures and brain damage, and cocaine can cause deadly heart attacks even in healthy young people.

The addict may also develop negative PERSONALITY traits, such as **paranoia,** the irrational belief that one is being persecuted. In addition, the addict may be unable to hold a job, keep up with schoolwork, or handle other everyday responsibilities. If the addict develops **tolerance,** or increased resistance to the substance, more and more of it is needed to keep the addict from feeling sick. This may lead to overdose and death.

The addict's family and friends and society as a whole pay a huge price for addiction. Addiction often leads to abuse and divorce, and it is also responsible for many lost workdays and half of all homicides, fatal car crashes, and suicides. In addition, many crimes are committed by addicts who cannot hold jobs and need money to support their habit.

Treatment of Addiction. There is no cure for addiction. Most experts recommend lifelong abstinence, or completely giving up the addictive substance or behavior. Treatment is aimed at helping the addict stay away from the drug or the harmful behavior. In cases of physical addiction to substances an initial period of **detoxification** may be needed to help the addict through any life-threatening medical problems, such as very high blood pressure, brought on by the sudden withdrawal of the substance.

PSYCHOTHERAPY can help many people with addictions by treating underlying mental health problems, such as depression or anxiety. Psychotherapy may also improve self-esteem and coping skills.

SUPPORT GROUPS can aid people in recovering from addiction by providing moral support and advice on dealing with day-to-day problems. Such groups include Alcoholics Anonymous (AA), for alcoholics; Alateen, for teens who have an alcoholic parent or other family member; and Narcotics Anonymous (NA), for people addicted to drugs such as heroin. Alternative treatments for

Keywords

detoxification withdrawal of an addictive substance under close medical supervision
paranoia irrational belief that others are out to harm you, a feature of some mental illnesses
tolerance capacity of the body to endure or become less responsive to a substance with repeated use

addiction include HYPNOSIS and RELAXATION THERAPY. Both help people cope with stress and reduce their need for addictive substances. [*See also* ABUSE AND MENTAL HEALTH; ALCOHOL AND MENTAL HEALTH; DRUG ABUSE AND MENTAL HEALTH.]

MORE SOURCES See www.alcoholics-anonymous.org; www.al-anon-alateen.org; www.na.org; www.niaaa.nih.gov

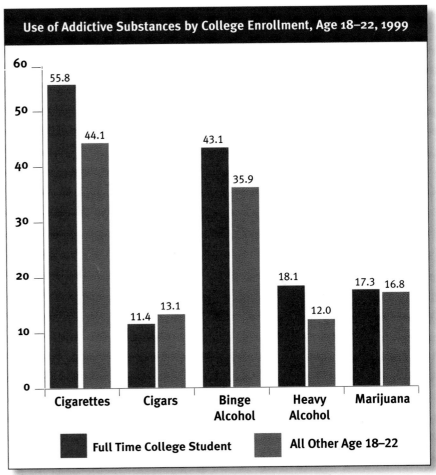

[Source: Substance Abuse and Mental Health Administration, 1999.]

ADJUSTMENT DISORDER A MENTAL ILLNESS in which reaction to a stressful event is more extreme or disruptive than is warranted. For example, a teen who is so upset after being turned down for a date that he misses a week of school may have adjustment disorder.

Symptoms of the condition include feelings of DEPRESSION or ANXIETY, physical health problems such as nausea or headaches, and changes in behavior. These conditions must last fewer than six months for the diagnosis of adjustment disorder to be made. If they last longer, they are probably not just an overreaction to a stressful event. Instead, they are more likely to be due to another mental illness, such as an ANXIETY DISORDER or depression.

Adjustment disorder does not always need treatment. Most people eventually get over the stressful event that triggered it. However, the disorder must be taken seriously because in some people, especially teens, it can lead to SUICIDE. Treatment of adjustment disorder includes PSYCHOTHERAPY to provide support for the patient and to help the patient learn techniques of STRESS MANAGEMENT. DRUG THERAPY for depression or anxiety may also be helpful.

AIDS AND MENTAL HEALTH *AIDS* (see Volume 7), or acquired immune deficiency syndrome, is an infectious disease caused by the human immun deficiency virus, *HIV* (see Volume 7). AIDS increases the risk of certain types of MENTAL ILLNESS. Some mental illnesses may also increase the risk of AIDS because they lead to risky behaviors.

AIDS and the Risk of Mental Illness. People with AIDS often develop DEPRESSION. Many people with AIDS also develop DEMENTIA, which is the loss of mental functions such as memory.

AIDS and Depression. AIDS is a life-threatening illness, and anyone who must cope with such an illness is at risk of becoming depressed. Medical problems, side effects of medication, financial concerns, and fear of dying all contribute to the risk.

Depression is characterized by feelings of intense sadness and worthlessness. Loss of appetite and difficulty concentrating are also common symptoms. These feelings can make it more difficult for people with AIDS to deal with their disease. For example, they may forget to take their medication or fail to eat enough to keep up their strength. People with depression are also at risk of taking their own lives. Fortunately, depression can usually be treated successfully with ANTIDEPRESSANTS.

AIDS Dementia. At least half of the people with AIDS eventually develop dementia. This usually occurs late in the disease. HIV can directly infect brain cells or, by destroying the immune system, lead to infections or tumors that kill brain cells. Some of the drugs used to treat HIV infection can affect brain cells and cause symptoms of dementia as well.

Symptoms of dementia include loss of memory, decrease in reasoning ability, inability to concentrate, confusion, and **disorientation**, which is loss of the sense of time or place. Physical weakness and **tremors**, or trembling, may develop as well. In addition, the person may show changes in personality, such as social withdrawal in a previously outgoing person. These symptoms tend to come on slowly. Eventually, however, the patient will no longer be able to speak or move.

Keywords

disorientation loss of the sense of time or place
tremors trembling or shaking

There is no cure for the dementia associated with AIDS. However, the use of memory aids, such as to-do lists and written schedules, may allow the patient with dementia to continue to function longer. Some medications, such as Cognex, may also temporarily help the patient concentrate and think more clearly.

Mental Illness and the Risk of AIDS. People with mental illness may be more likely to practice risky behaviors that increase their chances of HIV infection. For example, people who are suffering from depression or anxiety may abuse intravenous drugs in an effort to feel better. Those subject to certain PERSONALITY DISORDERS may be more likely to engage in unprotected sex. Both practices can increase the risk of becoming infected with HIV and developing AIDS.

ALCOHOL AND MENTAL HEALTH
Alcohol is the most commonly abused of all drug substances. People who abuse alcohol use it to the point that it causes problems in their lives. In many people alcohol abuse eventually leads to *addiction* (see Volume 1). People who are addicted to alcohol are called *alcoholics*. They need to drink every day just to feel comfortable physically and mentally. *alcohol abuse* (see Volume 1) and addiction can lead to MENTAL HEALTH PROBLEMS. Conversely, people with certain mental health problems are more likely to abuse alcohol and become alcoholics.

Rates of Alcohol Abuse and Addiction. Nearly 8 percent of all adults in the United States are alcohol abusers or addicts. About three-fourths of seniors in high school use alcohol. The earlier teens start to drink, the more likely they are to become alcoholics. Teens who start drinking in middle school may be alcoholics by the time they reach high school.

Risk Factors for Alcoholism. Several factors increase the risk of alcoholism. One is having a mental health problem such as DEPRESSION or ANXIETY. Many people with these conditions turn to alcohol in an attempt to lessen their emotional suffering. Having friends who drink supports the abuser's habit and the likelihood that alcoholism will develop. Because alcoholism tends to run in families, having a parent or other close relative who is addicted to alcohol also increases the risk.

Alcohol's Effects. Excessive use of alcohol can lead to serious health problems. Damage to the brain caused by alcohol can lead to DEMENTIA, a loss of memory and other mental abilities. It can also cause PSYCHOSIS, a loss of contact with reality. Long-term use of alcohol can lead to cirrhosis, a potentially fatal liver disease. In addition, alcohol can cause depression, a serious mental illness with a high risk of SUICIDE.

Alcohol's effects on society are equally great. It is involved in about one-half of all fatal car crashes, murders, suicides, and

Percentage of Binge Drinkers[a] Reporting Alcohol-Related Problems since the Beginning of the School by Gender		
ALCOHOL-RELATED PROBLEM	PERCENTAGE[b] WOMEN	MEN
General Disorientation		
HAVE A HANGOVER	81%	82%
DO SOMETHING YOU LATER REGRETTED	48	50
FORGET WHERE YOU WERE OR WHAT YOU DID	38	41
Sexual Activity		
ENGAGE IN UNPLANNED SEXUAL ACTIVITY	26	33
NOT USED PROTECTION WHEN YOU HAD SEX	15	16
Violence		
ARGUE WITH FRIENDS	29	32
DAMAGE PROPERTY	6	24
Disciplinary Action		
GET INTO TROUBLE WITH THE CAMPUS OR LOCAL POLICE	4	10
Personal Injury		
GET HURT OR INJURED	14	17
REQUIRE MEDICAL TREATMENT FOR A ALCOHOL OVERDOSE	<1	1
School Performance		
MISS A CLASS	42	45
GET BEHIND IN SCHOOL WORK	31	34

[a] Women binge drinkers report having four or more drinks in a row at least once during the last two weeks. Men binge drinkers report having five or more drinks in a row.
[b] Percentage of binge drinkers who report that, since the beginning of the school year, their drinking has caused them to experience each of the problems one or more times.
[Source: Harvard School of Public Health, *Alcohol Survey*, 1999.]

accidental deaths. Alcohol also contributes to MARITAL PROBLEMS, divorce, abuse, and absences from work. Teens who are alcoholics may steal alcohol or money to buy it. Instead of going to school, they may hide out and spend the day drinking. If they drive while drunk they may die in a car crash.

Treatment of Alcoholism. There is no cure for alcoholism. Most experts recommend total *abstinence* (see Volume 1) as the only way for alcoholics to recover. Most alcoholics suffer unpleasant withdrawal symptoms, such as anxiety and nausea, when they suddenly stop drinking after years of abuse. Some alcoholics experience life-threatening withdrawal symptoms, such as elevated blood pressure and racing heart. They must undergo up to a month of detoxification, or withdrawal from alcohol in a hospital or clinic.

Staying alcohol-free is extremely difficult for the majority of recovering alcoholics. PSYCHOTHERAPY may help by treating any mental health problems that are contributing to the addiction. Medications such as Antabuse can also be prescribed to help the recovering alcoholic stay sober.

The Twelve Steps of Alcoholics Anonymous

Alcoholic Anonymous (AA) is one group that helps people overcome alcohol addiction. AA recommends that its members practice these 12 steps as a way of life:

1. We admitted we were powerless over alcohol—that our lives had become unmanageable.

2. Came to believe that a Power greater than ourselves could restore us to sanity.

3. Made a decision to turn our will and our lives over to the care of God as we understood Him.

4. Made a searching and fearless moral inventory of ourselves.

5. Admitted to God, to ourselves and to another human being the exact nature of our wrongs.

6. Were entirely ready to have God remove all these defects of character.

7. Humbly asked Him to remove our shortcomings.

8. Made a list of all persons we had harmed, and became willing to make amends to them all.

9. Made direct amends to such people wherever possible, except when to do so would injure them or others.

10. Continued to take personal inventory and when we were wrong promptly admitted it.

11. Sought through prayer and meditation to improve our conscious contact with God as we understood him, praying only for knowledge of His will for us and the power to carry that out.

12. Having had a spiritual awakening as the result of these steps, we tried to carry this message to alcoholics and to practice these principles in all our affairs.

[Source: Alcoholics Anonymous, 2001.]

More alcoholics have been aided by SUPPORT GROUPS, particularly *Alcoholics Anonymous* (AA) (see Volume 1), than any other form of treatment. AA members come to accept that they are powerless against alcohol and that recovery is a lifelong process. They meet frequently to give each other advice and support as they struggle to remain alcohol-free.

Alternative Treatments. Alternative treatments that have been used for alcoholism include acupuncture and biofeedback. Research has demonstrated that both are about as effective as conventional medical treatments. When ALTERNATIVE MEDICINE treatments are used in conjunction with conventional treatments, the likelihood of recovery is even greater. [*See also* ABUSE AND MENTAL HEALTH; ADDICTION AND MENTAL HEALTH; DRUG ABUSE AND MENTAL HEALTH.]

ALTERNATIVE MEDICINE Methods and treatments that are not part of western, scientific medical practice. Alternative therapies include a wide range of practices that people use to treat a variety of ills. They fall into three broad groups: (1) those that have scientific evidence proving they are effective, (2) those that have scientific evidence proving they are not effective, and (3) those that experts are unsure about because the approaches have not yet been adequately studied. The first group of practices includes such things as relaxation therapy (for STRESS), biofeedback (for pain control), GROUP THERAPY (for psychological or emotional difficulties), HYPNOSIS (for behavioral ills), *yoga* (see Volume 4) (for stress), and drinking cranberry juice (for urinary tract infections). RELAXATION THERAPY and yoga involve the deliberate relaxing and tensing of muscles as well as MEDITATION exercises. Biofeedback is a method for mentally controlling some normal body processes (such as heart beat and blood pressure). It has also been used to treat alcoholism. Group therapy involves interaction among people who share common psychological problems. Psychiatrists and psychologists use hypnosis to powerfully suggest certain behaviors to patients.

The vast majority of alternative medical therapies falls into groups 2 and 3. For example, the use of vitamin C supplements to prevent the common cold has been scientifically proven to be ineffective. Scientists have not conducted enough research to determine the effectiveness of drinking green tea or eating the herb ginseng.

Scientific investigation of alternative medicine therapies is controversial. Proponents of alternative medicine say that scientists are often reluctant to study therapies that are so different from conventional medical treatments, so scientific evidence is lacking. Others say that science cannot properly assess alternative therapies at all because they work in ways that are too difficult for scientists to study. Most medical scientists disagree with this view because they have successfully conducted numerous studies on alternative treatments and gained important information about their safety and effectiveness. They say that the best way to assess alternative approaches is to apply the same scientific methods used in all other areas of medicine.

The National Institutes of Health (NIH) divides alternative practices into five major categories:

1. *Alternative Medical Systems*. These are complete systems of theory and practice that, in many cases, were devised independently of conventional scientific medicine. Often traditional parts of a culture, they encompass many kinds of treatment, including homeopathy, acupuncture, and naturopathy. In homeopathy a person takes small doses of a remedy that, in a healthy person, would produce symptoms of the disease being treated. Naturopathy

Fact or **Folklore?**

Folklore **Alternative medicine practitioners are "quacks" who prey on the uneducated.**

The term quacks refers to people who try to fool others into believing they have medical knowledge that they do not really possess or who use medical treatments that do not really treat illness. According to the National Institutes of Health, most alternative medical practitioners do have some sort of special knowledge that they believe is relevant to health. In addition, several alternative treatments, such as acupuncture and meditation, are known to be effective in treating illness. Further, studies show that well-educated people are more likely to use alternative medicine than people with less education, mainly because it lets them manage their own healthcare.

emphasizes that use of natural agents such as cold water, and heat, sunshine; and physical means such as manipulation of the body and electrical pulses.

Some addicts have found relief from addiction by use of acupuncture, a therapy in which tiny needles are placed at the trigger points of the body by a trained practitioner. Since 1996 the Food and Drug Administration (FDA) has approved the use of acupunction by licensed individuals. In the year 2000, scientists at Yale University reported success in treating addition to *cocaine* (see Volume 1) with auricular acupuncture, in which needles are placed in the outer ear. The researchers found that 55 percent of the subjects receiving this treatment were drug-free after eight weeks. Further studies are being conducted on this therapy.

2. Mind-body Interventions. These are techniques that attempt to affect the body's functions and symptoms by using the mind. These approaches include the use of meditation, hypnosis, dance, music, and prayer. The object is to achieve a certain mental state so that physical healing can begin. Hypnosis is an alternative remedy that has helped some people gain relief from their addictions, especially those who wish to give up smoking. When hypnotized, the person willingly enters a trancelike state and is given instructions that are intended to help them stop the addicting behavior. Patients can also be trained to perform self-hypnosis.

3. Biological-based Therapies. These practices are intended to directly affect the body's biological or chemical functions. In this group are therapies that involve eating herbs, certain foods, high-dose vitamins or minerals, and other naturally derived substances. Although there are few herbs proven to be effective in treating addiction, researchers of the National Center for Complementary and Alternative Medicine (NCCAM) are testing six chinese herb extracts as a possible treatment for alcoholism. Some experts believe that drugs such as St.-John's-wort, also used for treating DEPRESSION, may be effective in helping people end addictions. However, there is no scientific proof that this herbal drug actual works and the NIH reports that St.-John's-wort interferes with the function of several drugs, including some used to treat HIV, certian immunosuppressant drugs, cholesterol-lowering medications, cancer medications, seizure drugs, blood thinners, and birth-control pills.

4. Manipulative and Body-based Methods. These practices are intended to directly affect the body's biological or chemical functions. In this group are therapies that involve ingesting herbs, certain foods, high-dose vitamins or minerals, and other naturally derived substances.

5. Energy Therapies. These methods are intended to manipulate energy fields that can affect the body, some of which have not been scientifically proven to exist. Some of the most common energy therapies are therapeutic touch, Reiki, Qi gong, and the unconventional use of electromagnetic fields. Each focuses on a different kind of energy that allegedly flows from the body.

Alternative methods for treating MENTAL ILLNESS include light therapy for SEASONAL AFFECTIVE DISORDER, the herb St.-John's-wort for depression, hypnosis for ANXIETY DISORDERS, and fish oils for SCHIZOPHRENIA.

MORE SOURCES See www.nccam.nih.gov; www.quackwatch.com

ALZHEIMER'S DISEASE See DEMENTIA.

ANOREXIA See EATING DISORDERS.

ANTIDEPRESSANTS Drugs used to treat depressed moods and other MENTAL HEALTH PROBLEMS. There are many different antidepressants. The most commonly used are Zoloft, Paxil, and Prozac. Antidepressants were first developed to treat DEPRESSION. They have since been found to help people with other types of MENTAL ILLNESS as well, including ANXIETY DISORDERS, OBSESSIVE-COMPULSIVE DISORDER, and EATING DISORDERS.

Antidepressants and Depression. Antidepressants improve mood by increasing levels of either **serotonin** or **norepinephrine**, chemicals in the brain that help transmit messages between brain cells, also called **neurotransmitters**. It usually takes several weeks for antidepressants to start working and a couple of months for them to reach their maximum effect, but as many as 90 percent of depressed people are helped significantly by the drugs. The majority of people can stop taking antidepressants after 6–12 months. However, some people need to take low doses of the drugs for years to prevent the return of depressed moods.

The chance that a particular antidepressant will work for a given individual is about 65 percent. This is because different antidepressants vary somewhat in how they affect brain chemistry. Many people need to try more than one antidepressant before they find the one that works best for them. Those that tend to cause the fewest side effects are usually prescribed first.

Side Effects of Antidepressants. The most commonly used antidepressants cause few side effects, and the ones that they do sometimes cause, such as dry mouth and headache, are typically mild and short-lived. Other antidepressants can cause harmful side effects, such as high blood pressure or dizziness. Using these drugs also requires people to avoid certain foods and over-the-counter medications because they can cause dangerous interactions with the antidepressants.

Keywords

adrenaline hormone that stimulates the heart and other organs to prepare a person for fighting or fleeing from danger

neurotransmitters a substance that carries signals from one nerve from one cell to another

norepinephrine a hormone and a neurotransmitter that causes heart rate, blood pressure, and blood sugar levels to increase and the blood vessels to constrict, preparing the body to meet stressful challenges

serotonin a hormone and a neurotransmitter that helps transmit messages between cells, stimulate smooth muscles, and regulate learning, sleep and mood; found in the brain, blood, serum, and mucus membrane of the stomach

How Neurotransmitters Transmit Messages between Brain Cells

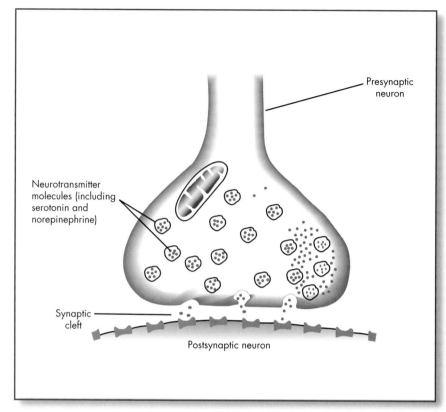

[Source: Cunningham, *Human Biology*, 1989.]

Most people with depression who take antidepressants find such relief from their emotional pain that they are willing to put up with the side effects. However, some people discontinue their medication for this reason. Although their mood may have improved, they risk relapsing into depression. [*See also* DRUG THERAPY.]

ANXIETY A nagging, uncomfortable feeling that something bad is about to happen. A low level of anxiety in certain situations is normal. For example, feeling worried the night before a big exam or being afraid of a dangerous animal is normal. Low levels of anxiety can help one perform better or avoid danger by heightening the senses and increasing concentration. However, if anxiety occurs for no reason at all or to a degree that is out of proportion to the cause, then it may cause physical illness or MENTAL HEALTH PROBLEMS. Up to a point, anxiety can actually improve performance. As anxiety increases, however, it causes distress and interferes with the ability to perform efficiently

People who are anxious tend to be restless, irritable, and tense. They may also have trouble falling asleep or suffer from such physical symptoms as stomachache, rapid heartbeat, headache, or tremors. Many people with anxiety turn to drugs or alcohol to try to calm their fears and mask their other symptoms.

Anxiety that lasts a month or more or disrupts daily life may be a symptom of an ANXIETY DISORDER. Anxiety may also point to other mental illnesses, such as DEPRESSION. In addition, some drugs, including alcohol and caffeine, can cause anxiety. Anxiety can be treated with RELAXATION THERAPY, antianxiety drugs, or alternative treatments such as MEDITATION. [*See also* DRUG THERAPY.]

ANXIETY DISORDERS A group of mental illnesses characterized by excessive worry or fear. They are excessive if they last for weeks or months, occur for no reason, or occur to a degree that is out of proportion to the cause. Excessive ANXIETY can cause physical symptoms such as rapid heartbeat by stimulating the production of **adrenaline**, the so-called "fight-or-flight" hormone. Anxiety conditions include PANIC DISORDERS, PHOBIAS, OBSESSIVE-COMPULSIVE DISORDER, and POSTTRAUMATIC-STRESS DISORDER.

Epidemiology. As a group, anxiety disorders are the most common type of MENTAL ILLNESS, affecting about 15 percent of

How Anxiety Affects Performance

[Source: Merck & Company, 1997.]

Americans. For unknown reasons anxiety disorders occur slightly more often in females than males and frequently begin in the teens.

Abnormal levels of brain chemicals, including norepinephrine and serotonin, seem to play a role in the development of anxiety disorders. The disorders often run in families, so the abnormalities may be inherited. Extremely frightening experiences, especially in childhood, may contribute to the development of anxiety disorders in people who are genetically at risk.

Anxiety Triggers. In generalized anxiety disorder anxiety is present most of the time without any trigger to set it off. In phobias, on the other hand, excessive fear of a particular object or situation causes the feeling. For example, a person with a fear of snakes might become anxious just hearing the word snake. Similarly, in posttraumatic-stress disorder anxiety occurs when the person is reminded of an extremely troubling event from the past. For example, a teen might become very anxious whenever she is reminded of a serious car crash she was in as a child.

In obsessive-compulsive disorder anxiety occurs because of **obsessions**, which are recurring disturbing thoughts or mental images. The intense anxiety the obsessions create can be relieved only by repeating certain ritualized behaviors, called **compulsions**. For example, many people with obsessive-compulsive disorder imagine that everything is crawling with germs. This obsession creates such tremendous anxiety that they feel compelled to relieve it by washing their hands over and over again.

Panic disorder is characterized by repeated **panic attacks**. A person has a sudden feeling of terror accompanied by physical sensations of fear. The heart suddenly starts racing, and there is a sensation of being unable to breathe. He or she may break out in a cold sweat and tremble. People with panic disorder have panic attacks for no apparent reason, but panic attacks may also occur in other anxiety disorders in response to a trigger. For example, someone with a phobia of spiders might have a panic attack when a spider crawls on his arm.

Treatment. Anxiety disorders can be treated with DRUG THERAPY and PSYCHOTHERAPY. A group of antianxiety drugs called *benzodiazepines*, which include Valium and Librium, can almost immediately quell anxious or panicky feelings. The drugs are addictive, however, so they must be used with caution. Another antianxiety drug, called Buspar, controls anxiety without being addictive, but it may take several weeks to begin working. ANTIDEPRESSANTS can also help control anxiety in some people.

Alternative Treatments. BEHAVIORAL THERAPY, a form of psychotherapy that helps patients change problem behaviors, is helpful for many people with anxiety disorders. In behavioral therapy for phobia, for example, the therapist helps the patient remain calm in the face of more and more intense contacts with the feared object until it no longer causes anxiety. RELAXATION THERAPY, MEDITATION, and massage may also help relieve symptoms of anxiety disorders.

ATTENTION DEFICIT HYPERACTIVITY DISORDER
(ADHD) A disorder characterized by inattention, hyperactivity, or both. People who are inattentive have difficulty concentrating and following directions, and they are easily distracted. Those who are hyperactive are impatient and always on the go, and they usually talk excessively.

Epidemiology. Between 5 and 10 percent of school-age children in the United States have ADHD. It occurs ten times more often in boys than in girls, but the reasons for this difference are not known. ADHD always appears in early childhood. If symptoms first show up after age seven, they are assumed to be due to some other condition or disorder.

The underlying biological cause of ADHD is an abnormality in brain chemistry. A tendency to develop the disorder is probably inherited, so it is likely to have a genetic basis. A stressful home or school environment may increase the chances of ADHD appearing in a child with the inherited brain abnormality.

What about Ritalin?

Drugs such as Ritalin can almost magically improve a child's behavior and school performance, but that improvement comes with a price. Ritalin and similar stimulants that are used to control ADHD cause unwanted side effects, such as loss of appetite and difficulty sleeping. Perhaps most disturbing is the possibility that long-term use of the drugs may interrupt normal growth. For these reasons some experts advise using the drugs only for severe cases and stopping the medications during summer vacations so children can catch up on their growth.

What Are the Signs of Attention-Deficit/Hyperactivity Disorder?

Children with the inattentive type:

- HAVE SHORT ATTENTION SPANS
- ARE EASILY DISTRACTED
- DO NOT PAY ATTENTION TO DETAILS
- MAKE LOTS OF MISTAKES
- FAIL TO FINISH THINGS
- ARE FORGETFUL
- DON'T SEEM TO LISTEN
- CANNOT STAY ORGANIZED

Children with the hyperactive-impulsive type:

- FIDGET AND SQUIRM
- ARE UNABLE TO STAY SEATED OR PLAY QUIETLY
- RUN OR CLIMB TOO MUCH OR WHEN THEY SHOULD NOT
- TALK TOO MUCH OR WHEN THEY SHOULD NOT
- BLURT OUT ANSWERS BEFORE QUESTIONS ARE COMPLETED
- HAVE TROUBLE TAKING TURNS
- INTERRUPT OTHERS

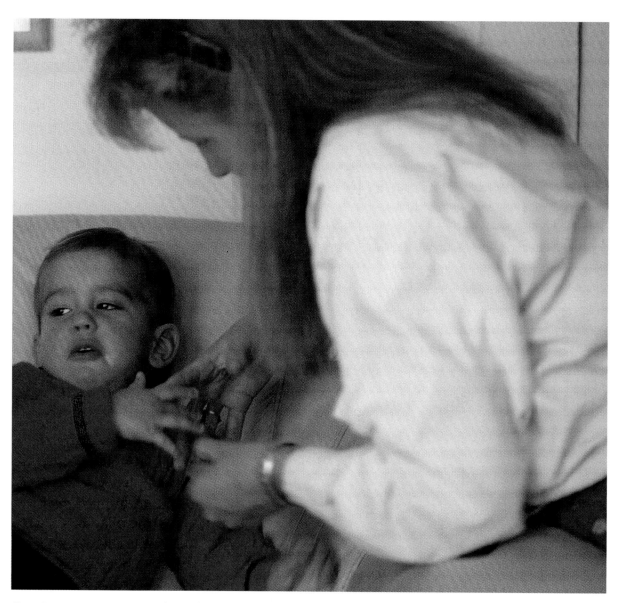

Parents may attempt to control poor behavior by offering "bribes" such as candy or gifts.

Diagnosing ADHD. For ADHD to be diagnosed, the inattention or hyperactivity must be serious enough to interfere with daily life. For example, lack of concentration or self-control in the classroom must be severe enough to cause poor grades or to disturb other students. The problems must also be characteristic of behavior in all settings—at home, in the classroom, and on the playground.

Some experts believe that many children are incorrectly diagnosed with ADHD just because they are very active or have short attention spans—traits that are normal for young children. Other people may be incorrectly diagnosed with ADHD because they are inattentive or hyperactive as a result of other MENTAL HEALTH PROBLEMS. For example, DEPRESSION, ANXIETY, and alcohol abuse can cause problems with concentration and make people restless.

Treatment. ADHD cannot be cured, but its symptoms can be managed with DRUG THERAPY and PSYCHOTHERAPY. Drug therapy, with or without psychotherapy, is usually recommended for people with severe ADHD. People with mild ADHD may be treated with psychotherapy alone.

Surprisingly, the drugs that work best to control ADHD are stimulants such as Ritalin. They calm hyperactivity and help the person focus. They also usually lead to improvement in school performance.

The psychotherapy method most often used to treat ADHD is BEHAVIORAL THERAPY. In behavioral therapy the therapist guides the patient in replacing problem behaviors, such as fidgeting, with more desirable behaviors, such as sitting still for relatively long periods of time. Parents and teachers are taught how to provide positive reinforcement for preferred actions both at home and at school.

> ## Fact or **Folklore ?**
>
> **Folklore** Attention deficit hyperactivity disorder is a childhood condition that is outgrown by adulthood.
>
> Although this used to be the accepted wisdom, scientists have recently determined that once you have ADHD, you probably have it for life. An estimated 65 percent of children diagnosed with ADHD continue to show at least some symptoms in adulthood.
>
> Usually, adults with ADHD are still inattentive but no longer hyperactive. They often lose things and forget to finish tasks just as they did in childhood, but they no longer have such a hard time sitting still or controlling impulsive behaviors.

B

BEHAVIORAL THERAPY A method of PSYCHOTHERAPY in which the therapist tries to help the patient modify problem behaviors. Behavioral therapy is widely used to treat most types of MENTAL ILLNESS, including DEPRESSION, EATING DISORDERS, and ANXIETY DISORDERS such as PHOBIAS.

Understanding Behavioral Therapy. Behavioral therapy is based on the premise that people can replace negative behaviors with positive ones if they are given reinforcement. For example, a child who is always disruptive at the dinner table might be given a special privilege, such as an extra half-hour of television time, each day that he or she does not disturb the meal. With consistent reinforcement of positive behavior the child should eventually show a permanent improvement in behavior.

Unlike some other methods of psychotherapy, behavioral therapy does not deal with the mind's inner workings or try to explore the childhood conflicts that may cause mental health problems. Instead, behavioral therapy focuses on changing the outward behavioral symptoms of mental health problems.

Behavioral Therapy for Depression. Behavioral therapy is commonly used to treat depression. One way is to encourage the depressed person to become more involved in social activities, because a person with depression tends to withdraw from social life, and the isolation makes the depression worse. The therapist might suggest that the teen make an effort to join a club at school or attend youth functions at the family's church or temple. As the teen becomes more involved with other people, the depressed mood is likely to improve.

Behavioral Therapy for Anxiety Disorders. Behavioral therapy is also commonly used to treat anxiety disorders, especially phobias, or irrational fears. Typically, the therapist trains the patient to respond more calmly to whatever triggers his or her anxiety. For instance, a person with a phobia of heights will be exposed to high places until he or she begins to feel more comfortable. People who suffer from other kinds of anxiety disorders can also be taught to respond more calmly to the objects or situations that trigger their anxiety.

BIPOLAR DISORDER A MOOD DISORDER in which episodes of DEPRESSION alternate with episodes of MANIA. People with bipolar disorder cycle back and forth between despair and elation, usually with periods of normal mood in between. About 25 percent of people with bipolar disorder attempt SUICIDE, virtually always during an episode of depression.

Epidemiology. Bipolar disorder affects 1–2 percent of Americans, occurring equally in both sexes. The disorder typically begins in the teens or early twenties and lasts for life. The earlier the illness begins, the more severe it tends to be.

Bipolar disorder is thought to be hereditary and caused by a genetic abnormality. It is much more likely to occur in someone who has a close biological relative with the disorder. In someone who has inherited bipolar disorder episodes of extreme mood may be triggered by such factors as STRESS or lack of sleep.

Symptoms. During an episode of depression people with bipolar disorder feel despair and may think about suicide. They are also likely to feel lethargic and worthless and to suffer from physical aches and pains. During an episode of mania they may feel so "high" that they think they are invincible. They may dash frantically about from one activity to another and talk nonstop. When they are manic, they are also likely to be behave impulsively—driving recklessly or spending money wildly, for example.

Episodes of depression usually last longer than episodes of mania. Episodes of normal mood, lasting from weeks to years, typically occur between mood extremes.

Treatment. Untreated, bipolar disorder tends to worsen through time, with more rapid shifts of mood and more extreme highs and lows. There is no cure for bipolar disorder, but the mood swings can be reduced in frequency and intensity with DRUG THERAPY and PSYCHOTHERAPY.

Mood-stabilizing drugs, such as lithium or Depakote, are almost always prescribed to help prevent mood swings and control episodes of mania. Drugs that have a calming effect, such as tranquilizers, may also be prescribed for mania. ANTIDEPRESSANTS are usually prescribed for depression.

In addition to drug therapy, psychotherapy is usually recommended for people with bipolar disorder. A major aim of this treatment is to help patients and their families understand the disorder and the need for continued drug therapy. Drugs must be continued for years and often for life to minimize the risk of recurrences. The drugs may have unpleasant or even dangerous side effects, so many patients discontinue taking them when they feel better despite the risk of relapse.

CENTERS FOR DISEASE CONTROL AND PREVENTION

(CDC) Federal agency in the U.S. Department of Health and Human Services that is responsible for investigating and helping to control diseases and disabilities. The CDC gathers data on the incidence of disease, helps determine the cause of epidemics and other health problems, and promotes ways to protect public health and prevent disease and disability. It also provides the latest information on diseases and public health to consumers, scientists, and government officials. The CDC maintains a dozen centers and offices that are concerned with different aspects of public health.

MORE SOURCES See www.cdc.gov

COGNITIVE THERAPY A type of PSYCHOTHERAPY that helps patients change distorted ways of thinking. Cognitive therapy is based on the assumption that negative thought patterns make people unhappy. The cognitive therapist tries to help patients realize that how they are thinking is a distortion of reality and guide them in adopting more realistic perceptions.

Cognitive therapy is commonly used to treat DEPRESSION. People suffering from depression tend to have negative thoughts about themselves and the world around them. They think they are worthless and responsible for everything bad that happens to them. For example, a woman who is so depressed that she can barely drag herself out of bed in the morning thinks she is a failure as a mother because she is not taking good care of her family. The cognitive therapist helps her see that her negative reaction is a symptom of her depression and not a reflection of her worth as a person.

Cognitive therapy is also commonly used to treat ANXIETY DISORDERS. People with anxiety disorders tend to "make mountains out of molehills." They have a "Chicken Little" way of thinking. For example, a teen might think he will never get into college after he fails one exam. The cognitive therapist might have the patient write down his thoughts about school, exams, and related subjects and then help him see how exaggerated his perceptions are. The therapist then guides the patient in replacing such thoughts with ones that are more in keeping with reality.

D

Keywords

denial refusing to see a difficult situation as it really is
dissociation mentally separating oneself from a stressful event
repression the burying of a painful memory or emotion

DEFENSE MECHANISMS Unhealthy ways of coping with painful situations and emotions. Specific defense mechanisms include dissociation, denial, repression, and acting out.

Dissociation is mentally separating oneself from a stressful event. For example, a person who experiences a near-fatal car crash may dissociate from the crash by losing her memory of it. However, every time she hears about another crash, she experiences great ANXIETY.

Denial is refusing to see a difficult situation as it really is. Many alcoholics are in denial that they have a drinking problem, for example. As a result, they do not see that they need to give up drinking, and they blame others for the problems their drinking creates.

Repression is burying a painful memory or emotion. For example, someone who experiences severe abuse as a young child may repress all memories of being abused. Although the memories are extremely painful, repressing them may lead to ANXIETY DISORDERS or DEPRESSION.

Acting out is behaving recklessly in order to avoid thinking about a stressful situation. A teen who is upset by a recent loss might act out by stealing a car for a joy ride. The reckless act is likely to create such a disturbance that it temporarily blots out the pain of the loss.

Defense mechanisms are unhealthy ways of coping because they allow people to mask their problems instead of facing them head on and trying to solve them. Although defense mechanisms may provide temporary relief from painful situations and emotions, in the long run they increase the chances of more serious MENTAL HEALTH PROBLEMS developing.

DEMENTIA Loss of memory and other mental abilities that interferes with daily functioning. Dementia usually starts slowly and progresses gradually. People with dementia become increasingly forgetful, especially about recent events. Their speech becomes hard to follow, and they have difficulty understanding what others say. Sooner or later they have trouble carrying out even simple tasks, such as brushing their teeth or tying their shoes. They may also experience personality changes. A previously easygoing, mild-mannered individual may become argumentative and aggressive.

Many people with dementia deny that they have a problem. They find it too frightening to face the loss of their mental functions. Other people with the condition become depressed or anxious because of the loss.

Causes of Dementia. Dementia is an organic brain disease. Its symptoms are due to the destruction of brain cells. The three leading causes of dementia are *Alzheimer's disease* (see volume 8), strokes, and *alcohol abuse* (see Volume 1). Dementia can also be caused by *Huntington's disease* (see Volume 8), *Parkinson's disease* (see Volume 8), and *HIV* (see Volume 7) infection. Dementia occurs most often after age 60, but it may occur at younger ages, especially in people with AIDS.

Treatment. Most cases of dementia are irreversible and continue to worsen over time. Nonetheless, people with dementia can be helped. In some cases memory loss can be slowed with a

Fact or Folklore?

Fact Becoming forgetful is a normal part of aging.

Most people experience a mild decline in memory as they age. Older people may be more likely to misplace their keys, for example, or have a harder time remembering a new phone number. However, their ability to function normally is not impaired. A decline in mental function that is severe enough to interfere with daily life is not a normal part of aging and may be a symptom of dementia.

VICTIMS OF DEPRESSION

About one in five people suffers from depression at some point in life. Each year 17 million Americans have the condition. Sadly, for nearly two-thirds of them their depression goes undiagnosed and untreated.

medication such as Cognex or Aricept. Symptoms of DEPRESSION can also be treated with ANTIDEPRESSANTS, and ANXIETY can be controlled with antianxiety drugs.

A stable, structured environment with a fixed daily routine may help the person with dementia continue to function longer. Simple devices, such as a large clock and calendar in an obvious place, can help prevent **disorientation** and allow the person with dementia to maintain a daily routine.

The caregivers of people with dementia must cope with a great deal of stress. Communication problems may lead to frequent misunderstandings, and the person with dementia may react with outbursts of temper. Eventually, loss of mental functions leaves the person with dementia completely helpless and in need of constant care. The caregiver must feed, bathe, and dress the patient and provide continuous supervision. Fortunately, SUPPORT GROUPS can help people cope with the stress of caring for a person with dementia. [See also AIDS AND MENTAL HEALTH; ALCOHOL AND MENTAL HEALTH.]

DEPRESSION A MOOD DISORDER characterized by long-lasting feelings of intense sadness. Most people, especially teens, have times when they feel sad. Such feelings are normal. For some people, however, feelings of sadness become almost unbearable and last for weeks, months, or even years. Those feelings are often accompanied by a sense of worthlessness and guilt. People who feel this way are suffering from depression.

Epidemiology. Depression is the single most common MENTAL ILLNESS. It is found equally in people of every socioeconomic level and ethnic background. It occurs in both males and females and in people of every age. It usually begins in late adolescence or early adulthood and is more common in females than males.

After childhood, females are twice as likely as males to be diagnosed with depression. This gender gap has been found in all parts of the world and at all levels of income and education. Why it occurs has been debated for years, and experts still have differing opinions. Some PSYCHOLOGISTS think that at least part of the gender gap may be due to an underestimate of depression in males, who are less likely to seek help when they are depressed. Others believe that the difference is real and due to the place of females in society. According to these experts, the socioeconomic status and gender roles of females increase their likelihood of low self-esteem and negative thinking, which in turn increase their risk of depression.

Causes of Depression. Depression is caused by a combination of genetic, biological, and psychological factors. Depression appears

Tips for Managing Your Depression

Do not expect too much from yourself too soon, as this will only accentuate feelings of failure. Avoid setting difficult goals or taking on new responsibilities.

Break large tasks into small ones, set some priorities, and do what can be done, as it can be done.

Recognize patterns in your mood. Like many people with depression, the worst part of the day for you may be morning. Try to arrange your schedule accordingly so that the demands are the least in the morning. For example, you may want to shift your meetings to midday or the afternoon.

Participate in activities that make you feel better. Try exercising, going to a movie or a ball game, or participating in religious or social activities. At a minimum, such activities may distract you from the way you feel and allow the day to pass more quickly.

You may feel like spending all day in bed, but do not. While a change in the duration, quality, and time of sleep is a core feature of depression, a reversal in sleep cycle (such as sleeping during daytime hours and staying awake at night) can prolong recovery. Give significant others permission to wake you up in the morning to decide what you will be doing during the day.

Avoid overdoing it or getting upset if your mood is not greatly improved right away. Feeling better takes time. Do not feel crushed if after you start getting better, you find yourself backsliding. Sometimes the road to recovery is like a roller coaster ride.

People around you may notice improvement in you before you do. You may still feel just as depressed inside, but some of the outward manifestations of depression will be receding.

Try not to make major life decisions (such as changing jobs or getting married or divorced) without consulting others who know you well and who have a more objective view of your situation.

Do not expect to snap out of your depression on your own by an exercise of will power. This rarely happens.

Remind yourself that your negative thinking is part of the depression and will disappear as the depression responds to treatment.

Find support from people who understand. Self-help groups can provide a supportive environment for you as well as your family and friends. Hospitals and health departments sponsor self-help groups, and an increasing number are found online.

[Source: Cheong, Herkov, and Goodman, *Tips for Managing Your Depression, 2001.*]

to run in families, so a tendency to develop the disorder may be inherited. The underlying biological cause of depression is low levels of the brain chemicals **serotonin** and **norepinephrine**, both of which help transmit messages between brain cells. When serotonin and norepinephrine are at lower than-normal levels, depression is more likely. Psychological factors, including low self-esteem and negative thinking, also appear to play a role in the development of depression.

Depression is a serious mental illness that is often treated with drug therapy.

In a person with a genetic, psychological, or biological tendency to develop depression a stressful event or serious loss, such as the divorce of parents or the death of a close relative, may trigger an episode of depression. In some people at high risk depression may occur even without such triggers.

Risk Factors. Going through a stressful event or serious loss is a risk factor for depression. Having experienced an episode of depression in the past increases the risk of having another occurrence. In fact, the more times one feels seriously depressed, the greater the risk that depression will strike again.

Because of the genetic link, having a family member with depression also increases the risk of the disorder. Suffering from a serious illness such as cancer or an addiction such as *alcoholism* (see Volume 1) increases the risk as well. In addition, certain medications, including sedatives and high-blood-pressure drugs, can heighten the risk of depression.

Signs and Symptoms of Depression. People experiencing depression feel as though nothing is pleasurable anymore. They often have no hope for the future. They also have a hard time concentrating and making decisions. They may withdraw from human contact and eventually lose all interest in life. As their quality of life decreases, they are likely to think often about death and SUICIDE.

Teens who are depressed may not feel or act sad. Instead, they may be irritable, impatient, and angry, especially toward their parents. Some depressed teens become destructive. For example, they may smash a hole in a wall with their fist. Other depressed teens become socially withdrawn. They may avoid old friends and spend almost all their time alone in their rooms.

People with depression are likely to have physical as well as emotional problems. They may lose their appetite or be ravenously hungry all the time and gain weight. They may suffer from sleepless nights or sleep far more than usual. They may feel too exhausted to move or too restless to sit still. Many people with depression also have aches and pains, upset stomachs, or constipation.

Death and Disability from Depression. About 15 percent of people with depression attempt to take their own lives; depression is the number-one cause of suicide in the United States. Even when depression does not kill, it is likely to cause disability because of its physical symptoms and the inability to concentrate, sleep, or make decisions. Depression ranks second only to advanced heart disease in the total number of days patients spend in the hospital or disabled at home.

Types of Depression. The most common types of depression are major depression and **dysthymia**. Far less common is SEASONAL AFFECTIVE DISORDER (SAD), a form of depression that occurs in some people when the days grow short in the winter. Also less common is POSTPARTUM DEPRESSION, a severe depression that occurs shortly after a woman gives birth.

Major Depression. Major depression is characterized by occurrences of the condition severe enough to cause difficulty working, sleeping, eating, or enjoying once-pleasurable activities. The episodes may last for weeks or months. This form of depression may occur from once to many times in a person's life.

Dysthymia. Dysthymia is less severe but longer lasting than major depression. A person with dysthymia does not have such intense feelings of sadness and guilt as a person with major depression, and the dysthymic person may be able to carry on with daily life. However, dysthymia usually begins earlier in life, typically in adolescence or childhood, and often lasts for many years or even for life. About half of the people with dysthymia also have episodes of major depression.

Prevention. Staying healthy and maintaining a positive attitude can help prevent depression. By eating a balanced diet, exercising regularly, and staying involved with family and friends, people are more likely to remain depression-free even if they are at risk. When an episode of depression does occur, it is likely to be less severe and last a shorter time if it is diagnosed early and treated quickly. Recognizing when one is at risk of depression can help in prompt diagnosis and treatment.

Treatment. Depression is one of the most treatable of all mental illnesses. Between 80 and 90 percent of depressed people improve with treatment. The most effective treatment for the majority of people is ANTIDEPRESSANTS. These are drugs, such as Prozac, Zoloft, and Paxil, that correct brain chemistry and alter mood. PSYCHOTHERAPY is often used in conjunction with antidepressants. It may help people change negative thoughts and behaviors that contribute to depression.

Another treatment for depression is **electroconvulsive therapy**, or ECT, in which an electric current is passed through the brain of the anesthetized patient. ECT is usually reserved for the small percentage of people who do not improve with other treatments. In cases of severe depression, especially when suicide is likely, hospitalization may be necessary until treatment is under way.

Alternative Treatments. Several alternative treatments are thought by some to be effective in relieving depression. The best known is St.-John's-wort, an herb that has been used to treat depression for centuries. *Aerobic exercise* (see Volume 4) is another widely used treatment. Both St.-John's-wort and aerobic exercise have been shown to change brain chemistry and improve mood in some depressed people.

Many people believe that the herb St.-John's-wort relieves some forms of depression and is a safe alternative to prescription drugs. Yet recent studies have shown that it does not seem to work against major depression. In addition the National Institutes of Health (NIH) noted that it might interfere with the effectiveness of several drugs, including some used to treat HIV, certain immuno-suppressant drugs, cholesterol-lowering medications, cancer medications, seizure drugs, blood thinners, and birth-control pills. Although the herb has become a self-treatment for depression, some physician's oppose its use at all until further studies can be done. [*See also* BIPOLAR DISORDER.]

MORE SOURCES See www.depression.com

DISSOCIATIVE DISORDERS
MENTAL ILLNESS in which dissociation occurs. *Dissociation* is a DEFENSE MECHANISM characterized by mentally separating oneself from a stressful event. For example, a teen who witnesses a gruesome murder may lose all memory of the bloodshed. Dissociative disorders include dissociative amnesia, dissociative identity disorder, and depersonalization disorder.

Dissociative Amnesia. Loss of memory is referred to as **amnesia**. In dissociative amnesia people forget stressful events that have occurred to them. However, memory of the events has been encoded in their brains and may still cause ANXIETY. A person who has lost the memory of driving off a bridge, for example, may become very anxious every time he has to cross a bridge.

Most people with dissociative amnesia do not need treatment, and the forgotten memories gradually return on their own. In some people, however, treatment is needed to help the patient remember and come to terms with the memories. HYPNOSIS has been used effectively for this purpose. Under hypnosis patients are guided in reviewing the forgotten events while imagining themselves in a safe environment. Because people are very suggestible while hypnotized, it is easy for the hypnotist to inadvertently "plant" false memories of events that never occurred. Therefore, hypnosis should be performed only by a skilled therapist.

Dissociative Identity Disorder. Formerly called *multiple personality disorder,* dissociative identity disorder is characterized by the existence of two or more personalities in a single individual. The disorder is most likely to develop in children who have suffered extreme abuse. People with this disorder have a high risk of SUICIDE.

Keywords

amnesia a complete or partial loss of memory

depersonalization uncomfortable feeling of being unreal or detached from one's body or surroundings

Each of the personalities has its own traits and attitudes. For example, one personality might be nearsighted, while another has perfect vision; or one personality might love jazz, while another likes only rock. Because the person keeps shifting from one personality to another, often without being aware of it, each personality also has different memories. The switching of personalities and loss of memories can make life chaotic for people with the disorder as well as for the people around them.

Dissociative identity disorder is usually treated with long-term PSYCHOTHERAPY, often including hypnosis. Typically, the goals of therapy are to bring all the personalities to the surface in a supportive environment and to join them together in an integrated whole. The therapist may literally introduce the patient to his or her other personalities while helping the patient deal with the anxiety that this creates.

Depersonalization Disorder. **Depersonalization** is an uncomfortable and sometimes scary feeling of being unreal or detached from one's body or surroundings. For example, a teen who is talking with a circle of friends may suddenly have the sensation that she is watching and listening to the others as an onlooker instead of as a participant. Occasional feelings of depersonalization are normal and do not necessarily indicate mental illness, although feelings of depersonalization also occur commonly in people who suffer from some mental illnesses, including DEPRESSION, POSTTRAUMATIC-STRESS DISORDER, and PANIC DISORDER.

Depersonalization disorder, however, is relatively uncommon. It is diagnosed when feelings of depersonalization are frequent, last for hours or days at a time, and cause great anxiety. The disorder may be treated with psychotherapy, MEDITATION, or hypnosis. DRUG THERAPY with tranquilizers or ANTIDEPRESSANTS can also help some people with the disorder. [*See also* ABUSE AND MENTAL HEALTH.]

DRUG ABUSE AND MENTAL HEALTH
Drug abuse is the harmful use of mind-altering substances. In teens this often takes the form of repeated drug binges. Many drug abusers eventually become drug addicts who are physically or psychologically dependent on drugs. The most commonly abused drug is alcohol. Others include nicotine, caffeine, prescription drugs, inhalants, and illegal drugs such as cocaine and heroin.

Epidemiology. Drug abuse is considered to be one of the greatest public health problems. Its health and financial costs are enormous. For example, one in ten Americans abuses alcohol, and alcohol-related diseases and accidents kill about 100,000 people in the United States each year. As many as 50 million Americans abuse nicotine. The economic costs of nicotine abuse far exceed $1 billion annually when one takes into account the cost of smoking-

Drugs That May Lead to Dependence

Drug	Psychologic Dependence	Physical Dependence
DEPRESSANTS (DOWNERS)	YES	YES
ALCOHOL	YES	YES
NARCOTICS	YES	YES
SLEEP AIDS (HYPNOTICS)	YES	YES
BENZODIAZEPHRINES	YES	POSSIBLY
INHALANTS	POSSIBLY	PROBABLY NOT
VOLATILE NITRATES	YES	YES
STIMULANTS (UPPERS)	YES	YES
AMPHETAMINE	YES	YES
METHAMPHETAMINE (SPEED)	YES	YES
METHYLENEDIOXYMETHAMPHETAMINE (MDMA, ECSTASY, ADAM)	YES	YES
COCAINE	YES	YES
2-5-DIMETHOXY-4-METHLAMPHETAMINE (DOM, STP)	YES	YES
PHENCYCLIDINE (PCP, ANGEL DUST)	YES	YES
HALLUCINOGENS	YES	YES
LYSERGIC ACID DIETHYLAMIDE (LSD)	YES	POSSIBLY
MARIJUANA	YES	POSSIBLY
MESCALINE	YES	POSSIBLY
PSILOCYBIN	YES	POSSIBLY

[Source: Merck, *The Manual of Medical Information*, 1997.]

related health problems. Almost two-thirds of American teens experiment with drugs, most often alcohol and nicotine, before they finish high school.

People who are mentally ill are more likely to abuse drugs than other people. They use drugs as a way to cope with their problems. Drug abuse makes existing MENTAL HEALTH PROBLEMS worse and creates even greater problems. People are also more likely to abuse drugs if the people around them do. In addition, having a close biological relative who abuses drugs increases the chances of developing addictive behavior, because drug abuse tends to run in families.

Effects of Drug Abuse. Drugs have a wide variety of physical effects. They range from the temporarily increased heart rate that occurs after drinking a soft drink loaded with caffeine to the serious liver and brain damage that follows years of abusing alcohol.

Intravenous drug abuse can lead to the spread of *AIDS* (see Volume 7), through the shared use of needles to inject drugs. *Alcohol abuse* can also lead to the spread of HIV and other sexually transmitted infections because people who are drunk are more likely to practice risky behaviors such as unprotected sex (see volume 1).

Drug abuse has negative psychological effects as well. Long-term use of cocaine, for example, can cause symptoms of DEPRESSION, and abuse of caffeine can lead to ANXIETY. Abuse of phencyclidine (PCP, or "angel dust"), which is an illegal anesthetic, can cause symptoms of PSYCHOSIS.

Treatment. Most experts agree that drug addicts must give up drugs entirely to be free of their dangers. However, withdrawing a potent drug after long-term use can create physical and psychological symptoms that are so unpleasant or painful that they often lead to relapse. For example, stopping alcohol abuse can cause **hallucinations** and seizures. Ending cocaine abuse can lead to depression so severe that SUICIDE is a serious risk. Withdrawal from heavy marijuana use can cause **tremors**, vomiting, and difficulty sleeping. Withdrawal of some drugs, particularly alcohol, may lead to potentially fatal withdrawal symptoms. As a result, many

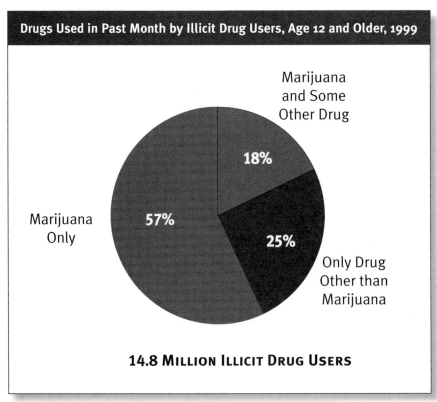

Drugs Used in Past Month by Illicit Drug Users, Age 12 and Older, 1999

Marijuana and Some Other Drug — 18%

Only Drug Other than Marijuana — 25%

Marijuana Only — 57%

14.8 MILLION ILLICIT DRUG USERS

[Source: Substance Abuse and Mental Health Services Administration, 1999.]

abusers must undergo **detoxification**, or medically supervised withdrawal from the drug.

Once the drug is out of their system, former abusers usually need help abstaining from the drug for life. GROUP THERAPY may be recommended to help them understand why they abused drugs and how they can avoid abusing them again. Many people who abuse drugs have underlying mental health problems that also need to be treated. People who drink because they are depressed, for example, may have less need for alcohol if their depression is lifted with ANTIDEPRESSANTS.

SUPPORT GROUPS such as Alcoholics Anonymous (AA) and Narcotics Anonymous (NA) play an important role in helping many former drug abusers remain drug-free. Group members provide each other with moral support and advice on coping with life without drugs, and older members show new ones by their example that it is possible to remain drug-free. [See also ABUSE AND MENTAL HEALTH; ADDICTION and MENTAL HEALTH; ALCOHOL and MENTAL HEALTH; MENTAL ILLNESS.]

DRUG THERAPY Use of medications to treat illness. Most types of MENTAL ILLNESS can be treated with drug therapy. Some mental illnesses, such as DEPRESSION, can often be treated successfully with drug therapy alone because they almost always have a biological basis. Other mental illnesses, such as EATING DISORDERS, are usually treated with a combination of drug therapy and PSYCHOTHERAPY because they are usually caused by a complex mix of biological and psychological factors.

Types of Drugs Used for Mental Illness. The drugs most commonly used to treat mental illness are ANTIDEPRESSANTS. Others often applied are antianxiety drugs, antipsychotic drugs, and mood stabilizers.

Antidepressants. Antidepressants, including Prozac, Paxil, and Zoloft, are the most widely used drugs in the United States. They help improve depressed mood and calm feelings of ANXIETY. Antidepressants are prescribed for depression and other MOOD DISORDERS, eating disorders, ANXIETY DISORDERS, and drug abuse.

Antianxiety Drugs. Antianxiety drugs include Valium, Halcion, and Buspar. They work to quell fears and relieve symptoms of panic and excessive worry. They are prescribed for people with PANIC DISORDERS, PHOBIAS, and other anxiety disorders.

Antipsychotic Drugs. Antipsychotic drugs, such as Thorazine, Zeldoc, and Risperdal, relieve symptoms of PSYCHOSIS, which can be caused by alcohol abuse, severe depression, SCHIZOPHRENIA, or DEMENTIA. Common psychotic symptoms include **delusions**, or

Keywords

delusions false beliefs
detoxification withdrawal from an addictive substance under close medical supervision
hallucinations false perceptions
tremors trembling or shaking

false beliefs, and hallucinations, or false perceptions. For example, someone who is psychotic might think she has superhuman powers and hears voices telling her what to do.

Mood Stabilizers. Mood stabilizers, such as lithium, Depakote, and Haldol, are prescribed for BIPOLAR DISORDER. People with this disorder swing wildly from the depths of depression to the heights of MANIA, or excessively elevated mood. Mood stabilizers help prevent these mood swings as well as control periods of mania.

Side Effects. Most drugs used to treat mental illness have side effects. These may range from mild to life-threatening. Antidepressants can cause loss of interest in sex, for example, and most antianxiety drugs are addictive. Antipsychotic drugs can cause severe uncontrollable **tremors**, and mood stabilizers can cause diarrhea. Because of side effects such as these, many people who are mentally ill discontinue drug therapy before they should, and their symptoms often return as a result.

EATING DISORDERS Mental illnesses in which eating behaviors are abnormal and unhealthy. *Eating disorders* (see Volume 4) include anorexia nervosa and bulimia nervosa. Both can be fatal because they may cause life-threatening health problems. People with both types of eating disorders are also at high risk of committing SUICIDE.

Epidemiology. Eating disorders almost always begin during adolescence, and at least 90 percent of people with them are female. In our society teenage girls are bombarded with the message that "thin is beautiful." Super-thin models grace magazine covers, and popular female singers appear to spend more time at the gym than the recording studio. At the same time, fattening food is available everywhere, and the majority of people overeat. This combination leads many teenage girls to develop eating disorders.

Eating disorders are not just about losing weight. The abnormal eating patterns are really a symptom of an underlying problem with body image. People with eating disorders are deeply dissatisfied with their bodies. At the same time, they are convinced that with enough willpower they can change themselves physically to conform to the ideal of thinness. Low self-esteem and DEPRESSION may contribute by making girls feel worthless. Controlling what they eat and how much they weigh may also give them a sense of control they have never experienced in other areas of their life.

Anorexia Nervosa. People with anorexia nervosa compulsively starve themselves until they are dangerously thin. They may also exercise excessively. The illness typically starts out with cutting back on food to lose a few pounds. The dieting gets out of control, and maintaining a thin body soon becomes the sole focus of existence. Despite their low weight, people with anorexia nervosa still think of themselves as fat, and they usually deny that they have a problem. They may suffer serious symptoms of malnutrition, such as weakness, dehydration, and potentially fatal abnormal heart rhythms. Females with the disorder also stop having menstrual periods.

Bulimia Nervosa. People with bulimia nervosa binge on huge amounts of food and then purge themselves of the food by vomiting or abusing laxatives. The disorder typically develops in people whose efforts to diet are so stringent that they lead to food binges. The binges cause them to feel guilty and anxious about gaining weight, so they purge. Soon, repeated cycles of binging and purging come to dominate their lives.

Although their weight tends to remain around average, the repeated purging wreaks havoc on the body. Vomiting of strong stomach acids can eventually corrode tooth enamel, inflame the salivary glands, and cause ulcers of the esophagus. Loss of fluids through vomiting and purging can reduce the level of potassium in the blood and lead to potentially fatal disturbances of heart rhythm.

Treatment. The first step in treating anorexia nervosa is weight gain. Hospitalization may be necessary to ensure that the patient eats, because people with the disorder will do almost anything to avoid eating and gaining weight.

COGNITIVE THERAPY or BEHAVIORAL THERAPY is also usually recommended for people with eating disorders. Behavioral therapy uses positive reinforcement to change abnormal eating behaviors. For example, a teen with anorexia nervosa might be rewarded with extra television or phone time for each pound she gains. Cognitive therapy aims at changing distorted thinking about food and body image. A teen with bulimia who thinks that eating one cookie will make her fat will be shown how irrational her thinking is so she can adopt a more realistic outlook.Because many people with eating disorders also suffer from depression, ANTIDEPRESSANTS may be prescribed to help elevate their mood.

EPIDEMIOLOGY Study of the distribution of and factors that cause diseases and other health problems in groups of people. It is epidemiologists—scientists who are experts in epidemiology—who usually discover the causes behind specific types of diseases, injuries, and medical conditions.

Think about It!

How Not to Control Your Weight
Vomiting once in a while after you have overeaten may seem like a harmless way to control your weight. You may know teens who do it, or perhaps you have thought about doing it yourself. Be aware that the behavior can become compulsive and quickly lead to bulimia nervosa. Then it not only makes your life miserable; it may also destroy your health and even kill you.

Epidemiologists conduct studies that involve making observations and collecting data of many people who may have been, or who may be, victims of mental disorders, diseases, or conditions. Sometimes an epidemiological study may deal with something as simple as trying to determine the mortality or death rate associated with a type of disease among a specific group or population—for instance, how many people between ages 18 and 21 die as a result of suicide.

More often, epidemiological studies involve searching for complex links or connections between diseases and other factors. Scientists who conduct such studies, for example, may discover that a certain food additive is associated with nervous disorders such as *Parkinson's Disease* or *Alzheimer's Disease* (see Volume 8). This finding becomes a strong clue, although not proof, that the additive can cause disorders of the nervous system. A study like this would then lead to more research. The study may be repeated to make sure that no errors in observations or in the collection of data were made, and similar studies may be conducted to look more closely at the links between Parkinson's and Alheimer's. If enough epidemiological studies achieve the same results, and the association is strong and consistent, scientists may conclude that the additive is not just associated with the disorders, but may causes it. Such an understanding may lead to better ways of prevention.

FAMILY ABUSE AND MENTAL HEALTH See ABUSE AND MENTAL HEALTH.

FAMILY THERAPY A type of PSYCHOTHERAPY in which family members are treated together as a group. Family therapy is the most common form of GROUP THERAPY. Usually, one member of the family has a MENTAL HEALTH PROBLEM or MENTAL ILLNESS that leads to therapy, and other family members are later brought into treatment as well.

Family therapy may be needed if family relationships are contributing to the patient's problems. For example, a teen may have developed low self-esteem because her parents often criticize her in a belittling way. Family therapy would help the parents see how their words affect their child and how they can communicate their concerns in a more positive way.

Sometimes family members need help coping with the effects of the patient's mental illness on their own lives. For example, family members of people suffering from DEMENTIA may seek family therapy to help them deal with the loss of mental function and the negative personality changes that are characteristic of the condition.

Family therapy can also be useful in helping family members better understand the patient's mental illness and its treatment. For example, controlling BIPOLAR DISORDER requires lifelong DRUG THERAPY, which may have unpleasant side effects, such as tremors and weight gain. Family therapy can help the patient's family appreciate the need for treatment and learn ways to help the patient continue with drug therapy.

MORE SOURCES See www.aamft.org

GENERALIZED ANXIETY DISORDER (GAD) See
ANXIETY DISORDERS.

GRIEF The normal emotional and physical response to a loss. The most common cause of grief is the death of a loved one. People also experience grief after the breakup of a serious romantic relationship or marriage.

Stages of Grief. Most people who are grieving go through four stages of grief. Some people move through the stages in just weeks or months, but many people take a year or more to recover from their loss. This is especially likely if they suffered a devastating loss, such as the unexpected death of a parent or spouse.

Denial. At first, people who are grieving may have a hard time believing that the death or other loss really happened. They may be emotionally numb and not yet feel much pain because they are in a state of shock. They may also find it difficult to concentrate or think clearly.

Despair. After a few days or weeks most people who are grieving face the reality of the loss. This is when they also start feeling a great deal of emotional pain. Many people also feel anger in this stage of grief and lash out at those around them.

Fact or Folklore?

Folklore It is better to "keep a stiff upper lip" when suffering a loss than to give in to your grief.

Grieving is not only normal after a serious loss but also the healthiest way to deal with the loss. People who fail to grieve do not come to terms with the loss, and they are likely to express their pain in other ways. For example, they may develop aches and pains that mimic the physical symptoms suffered by the deceased before death. Continued refusal to deal with the reality of the loss is called absent grief reaction. People with absent grief reaction may need PSYCHOTHERAPY to help them face the loss and process their grief.

Depression. As time passes, the raw pain of despair settles into feelings of deep sadness. During this stage people who are grieving may have little interest in life and find no pleasure in things they once enjoyed. They may also have trouble sleeping, lose their appetite, or feel tired all the time. They may withdraw socially, as well, which can make their emotional state even worse.

Someone who still feels this way months after a loss or who feels suicidal or guilty about the loss is likely to be suffering from major DEPRESSION. This is a MENTAL ILLNESS and not a normal response to grief. It should be treated promptly. Health-care providers treat depression with ANTIDEPRESSANTS or PSYCHOTHERAPY.

Resolution and Acceptance. After months of painful emotions most people who are grieving finally start to feel better. They have more energy, they can talk about the deceased without crying, and they begin to enjoy themselves once again. However, the sense of loss is likely to persist indefinitely. When this stage ends, they have not really "gotten over" the loss, but they have made sense of it and are ready to go on with their lives.

Coping with Grief. There is no treatment for grief other than time. Nonetheless, people who are grieving may benefit from outside help. Sources of help include SOCIAL SUPPORT SYSTEMS, SUPPORT GROUPS, and psychotherapy. If someone you know is grieving, you can help by staying in touch, offering help and support, and being a good listener.

GROUP THERAPY A type of PSYCHOTHERAPY in which several of people who share a common problem are treated together by a therapist. The most common form of group therapy is FAMILY THERAPY, in which the group consists of members of the same family. Many different MENTAL HEALTH PROBLEMS and types of MENTAL ILLNESS are treated with group therapy, including alcoholism and PERSONALITY DISORDERS.

The first method of group therapy that was developed was *psychodrama*. It is still widely used today. In this approach patients act out their problems on a stage. The therapist is the director who assigns patients their roles and suggests how they might act. For example, a teen might act out a scene from childhood, with other group members playing the roles of parents and siblings. The process helps people become more aware of their problems and how they might change their behavior.

For many people group therapy is more effective than individual therapy. Being part of a group takes pressure off the patient. Members of the group can also give each other moral support and insights based on their experiences with the illness. Just knowing that other people share the same problem can be an important benefit of group therapy for many people.

In group therapy, patients share experiences under the guidance of a therapist.

HYPNOSIS A sleeplike state induced by suggestion. Hypnosis is used in PSYCHOTHERAPY to treat a variety of MENTAL HEALTH PROBLEMS and types of MENTAL ILLNESS, including addictions and ANXIETY DISORDERS. To be successfully hypnotized, a person must be able to concentrate and trust the therapist.

Hypnosis helps people relax and focus more clearly on their problems. It can also change how they perceive pain, which makes it useful for treating severe or chronic pain. In addition, hypnosis can help people control how they respond mentally and physically to stress and the things that they fear.

IRRATIONAL BEHAVIOR Actions, deeds, or words that are considered different or unusual in a person who does not normally exhibit those characteristics. Irrational behavior may be a symptom of several conditions. For example, it could indicate *alcohol*

abuse (see Volume 1), illegal *drug abuse* (see Volume 1), or a negative reaction to a prescription medication. It may also be symptomatic of physical conditions such as malnutrition caused by vitamin B-12 deficiency, dehydration, infection, or a head injury, especially in older people. Irrational behavior is also seen in Alzheimer's patients. A physician or mental healthcare professional should evaluate individuals who exhibit any irrational behavior.

L

LAWS AND MENTAL ILLNESS Two important legal issues relate to MENTAL ILLNESS. One is whether people who are mentally ill should be forced to receive treatment. The other issue is whether people with mental illnesses should get the same health insurance coverage as people with physical illnesses.

Involuntary Treatment Laws. The issue of forcing mentally ill people to receive treatment has been debated since the 1960s. At that time there was an attempt to shift the treatment of the mentally ill away from hospitals to community mental health centers and clinics. Unfortunately, not enough money was provided to fund community care, and this resulted in no care at all for many patients. Other patients refused or discontinued treatment because of side effects of DRUG THERAPY or because they were too ill to be responsible for their own care. For the sickest patients, who were unable to function without treatment, lack of care often led to homelessness, substance abuse, and crime.

Some experts have argued that the mentally ill should be forced to receive treatment for their own good as well as for the good of society. Other people have reasoned that to compel the mentally ill to receive treatment against their will is an infringement of their civil rights and could drive them away from seeking voluntary treatment. Nonetheless, by the year 2000 the majority of states had passed laws forcing mentally ill people into treatment. However, some of these laws are being challenged in the courts because of the civil rights implications.

Mental Health Parity Act. Traditionally, less health insurance coverage was provided for mental illnesses than for physical illnesses. In part this was because older forms of treatment for mental illness typically involved costly PSYCHOTHERAPY that lasted many months or even years. Increased understanding of the biological basis of mental illness and the development of effective drug

Movements in Mental Health Treatment in the U.S.			
Reform Movement	**Era**	**Setting**	**Focus of Reform**
MORAL TREATMENT	1800–1850	ASYLUM	HUMANE, RESTORATIVE TREATMENT
MENTAL HYGIENE	1890–1920	MENTAL HOSPITAL OR CLINIC	PREVENTION, SCIENTIFIC ORIENTATION
COMMUNITY MENTAL HEALTH	1955–1970	COMMUNITY MENTAL HEALTH CENTER	DEINSTITUTIONALIZATION, SOCIAL INTEGRATION
COMMUNITY SUPPORT	1975–PRESENT	COMMUNITY	MENTAL ILLNESS AS A SOCIAL WELFARE PROBLEM (HOUSING, EMPLOYMENT)

[Source: U.S. Surgeon General, 1999.]

therapy led to pressure to provide equal insurance coverage for the mentally ill. In response the Mental Health Parity Act was passed in 1996. It guaranteed mental patients the same insurance rights as patients with physical illnesses. [*See also* MENTAL ILLNESS AND CRIME.]

MORE SOURCES See www.nami.org

MANIA Inappropriate or prolonged period of excitement and hyperactivity. Mania is not a MENTAL ILLNESS itself but a symptom of a mental illness called BIPOLAR DISORDER. Formerly known as *manic-depressive illness*, bipolar disorder is one of several MOOD DISORDERS. It is characterized by repeated cycles of mania and DEPRESSION.

People who are manic often feel euphoric, or on top of the world. They have unbelievable amounts of energy and go for days with little or no sleep. They may talk nonstop or accomplish incredible amounts of work. However, they are also likely to have poor judgment, and the work they do is unlikely to be as good as they think it is. In addition, people who are manic tend to be impulsive. For example, they may jet to another continent on the spur of the moment.

Mania cannot be cured. Once a person has one episode of mania, it is likely that he or she will have more occurrences. However, manic outbreaks can be brought under control and often prevented with drugs called *mood stabilizers*, which include lithium, Depakote, and Tegretol. The drugs usually must be continued for life. [*See also* DRUG THERAPY.]

MARITAL PROBLEMS Troubles in the relationship between husband and wife. Common marital problems center on money, sexuality, in-laws, and childrearing. They are likely to be worse if the husband or wife is unable to compromise or has trouble communicating. Marital troubles occur in the majority of marriages. Many people resolve their problems, but marital upsets also frequently lead to separation or divorce.

Risk Factors. Some marriages are at greater risk of marital problems than others. Risk factors include knowing each other for only a short time before marriage, having a low level of education or income, and having been married before. Couples in which the husband and wife come from different ethnic or religious backgrounds are also at a higher risk of marital problems.

Warning Signs. There are several possible warning signs that a marriage has problems. One is an increase in arguments, especially angry, hostile exchanges. Another is a decline in shared activities, affection, or intimacy. A third is one or both partners feeling lonely, neglected, or misunderstood.

Marital Problems and Mental Health. Marital problems are more likely in marriages in which one or both partners have MENTAL HEALTH PROBLEMS, such as substance abuse, or a MENTAL ILLNESS, such as DEPRESSION. Conversely, marital problems may lead to mental health problems or make them worse. For example, men and women who are divorced have higher rates of depression than people who are happily married. For women a bad marriage is more damaging than no marriage at all, because unhappily married women have even higher rates of depression than divorced women.

Children of unhappily married couples are also at risk of mental health problems. When parents fight frequently, children may become depressed and anxious. They may fear their parents will divorce, and this can cause a great deal of insecurity. Children of feuding couples often think they are responsible for the difficulties between their parents, leading to feelings of guilt. Unfortunately, many couples make the problem worse by trying to get the children to take sides in their battles with each other.

The Role of Communication. The most common marital problem is poor communication. Sheer lack of talking is part of the

Family therapy is often required when a couple is having marital problems.

problem. The average married couple talk together for just four minutes each day. How couples communicate is another part of the problem. Couples may communicate in ways that make their problems worse instead of better. For example, they may constantly criticize and blame their partner or always interrupt when their partner tries to talk. The partner, in turn, may become defensive and either counterattack or withdraw emotionally.

Help for Marital Problems. Recognizing that a marriage has problems and taking steps to resolve them can make both partners happier and healthier and may even may save the marriage from divorce. Improving communication is usually a good place to start. Couples can improve their communication by becoming better listeners and responding with "I" statements that express empathy ("I can see how upset that made you") rather than "you" statements that express criticism or blame ("You were stupid to do that"). Couples can also try to stay focused on the problem at hand instead of bringing up past mistakes. In addition, they can try to be assertive about their wants and needs without becoming angry or hostile.

Often couples with marital problems can be helped with some type of PSYCHOTHERAPY, such as MARITAL THERAPY, either individually or together. When children are involved, FAMILY THERAPY may be the best alternative. [See also ABUSE AND MENTAL HEALTH; ADDICTION AND MENTAL HEALTH; ALCOHOL AND MENTAL HEALTH.]

MARITAL THERAPY Type of PSYCHOTHERAPY in which the therapist tries to help a couple resolve MARITAL PROBLEMS. Marital therapy helps couples develop the skills and attitudes needed for a healthy relationship, such as good communication skills and a willingness to compromise. Unlike some other forms of psychotherapy, marital therapy is typically short term, usually lasting a year or less, because it is focused on specific problems.

Types of Marital Therapy. Most often, marital therapy involves both partners going to the same therapist together, but sometimes only one partner is willing to undergo therapy, or the partners go to different therapists. Some marital therapists hold GROUP THERAPY sessions in which several couples meet together with one or two therapists.

Role of the Therapist. In marital therapy the therapist acts as a mediator. As an impartial outside observer, the therapist can help the couple see how their relationship works and identify specific problems. The therapist can also guide the couple in reaching compromises by helping each partner see things from the other's point of view.

MORE SOURCES See www.health-center.com

MEDITATION An ALTERNATIVE MEDICINE technique in which the mind is used to control the body. Meditation has been practiced for thousands of years in many different cultures and in several major religions, including Hinduism and Buddhism. Today millions of people worldwide use meditation as a way of relaxing and improving their overall well-being.

Meditation commonly involves sitting comfortably on a chair or cushion, relaxing the body, breathing slowly, and concentrating on an object, such as a candle or flower. At the same time, the person tries to shut out distracting thoughts. Usually this continues for a short period of time and is repeated each day.

A somewhat different form of meditation, called *transcendental meditation* (TM), was developed in the 1960s. In TM people chant a special word, called a *mantra*, instead of concentrating on an object. Another form of meditation, called *yoga* (see Volume 4), originated in India several thousand years ago. In yoga people assume and hold special postures, or positions, while they control their breathing and meditate.

Meditation usually leaves people feeling more relaxed and focused. It can help relieve STRESS, lower blood pressure, induce sleep, and make pain more tolerable. Meditation can also help relieve PANIC DISORDER and DEPRESSION.

MENTAL HEALTH The ability to cope with stressful experiences and losses in healthy ways. If you have good mental health, you are able to work through life's normal transitions and crises without falling apart. In fact, if you have good mental health, such experiences can help you grow emotionally.

Indicators of Mental Health. What is considered good mental health in one culture may be considered poor mental health or even MENTAL ILLNESS in another. In some cultures, for example, it is considered normal to react to the death of a loved one without showing any emotion, while in other cultures it is considered normal to wail and cry publicly.

Despite such cultural variations, there are certain traits that reflect good mental health in any culture. They include the ability to fulfill one's roles and responsibilities, accept and like oneself, maintain relationships with other people, perceive others realistically, and think rationally.

Fulfilling Roles and Responsibilities. Good mental health means being able to accept responsibilities and function in society. For example, mentally healthy teens can handle chores at home and work at school without becoming excessively stressed. They may not always want to get up for school every day or cut the grass on the weekend, but they accept and fulfill these responsibilities.

Accepting Oneself. Another trait of people with good mental health is self-acceptance. Although they may not be happy with every detail about themselves, they still like and value themselves overall. For example, they may not like their teeth or their hair, but they think they are attractive and worthwhile despite their perceived flaws.

Maintaining Relationships. People with good mental health usually get along with others, and they stay actively involved with other people. They are not necessarily the most popular people in school or the life of the party, but they care about and interact with other people rather than spend all their time alone.

Perceiving Others Realistically. Another trait of good mental health is having realistic perceptions of other peoples' behaviors and motives. People with good mental health do not assume that someone is out to get them when things go wrong. They give other people the benefit of the doubt and do not greet new people with suspicion and distrust. On the other hand, mentally healthy people also realize that people can be untrustworthy, selfish, or cruel. Nonetheless, they are able to maintain a healthy skepticism without becoming paranoid.

Thinking Clearly. People with good mental health think logically and rationally, and their ideas are reasonable. When they talk with other people, they make sense and do not jump haphazardly from one topic to another.

Mental Health and Happiness. Being mentally healthy does not mean being happy all the time. Everybody has disappointments and losses that cause unhappiness. Reacting to disappointments and losses any other way would not be normal. However, people with good mental health are able to bounce back from setbacks and go on with their life.

MORE SOURCES See www.nimh.nih.gov

MENTAL HEALTH PROBLEMS Thoughts and behaviors that negatively affect MENTAL HEALTH. Mental health problems include low self-esteem, ANXIETY, and reliance on DEFENSE MECHANISMS. Problems such as these are not considered to be mental illnesses, but they can increase the risk of MENTAL ILLNESS developing.

Low Self-esteem. People with low self-esteem have a poor opinion of themselves and blame themselves when things go wrong. They typically lack self-confidence, are easily hurt by other people, and often feel powerless. Such feelings, many experts believe, increase the risk of DEPRESSION, which is the single most common mental illness.

Many teens, especially females, have low self-esteem. In part this is because our culture places so much emphasis on physical appearance. Most teenage girls do not match the ideal of beauty represented by the models they see in catalogs or the entertainers they see on television. This leads them to feel unattractive and lowers their self-esteem.

Anxiety. Anxiety is a feeling of dread or nagging worry. Feeling anxious in a dangerous situation is normal and may help protect one from harm. However, when anxiety is out of proportion to the cause, or when it occurs for no reason, it becomes a mental health problem.

Severe anxiety can distract people and prevent them from concentrating. It may rob them of sleep and cause them to do poorly at school or work. Continued high levels of anxiety may lead to depression or ANXIETY DISORDERS.

Keywords

denial refusing to see a difficult situation as it really is

repression the burying of a painful memory or emotion

norepinephrine a hormone and a neurotransmitter that causes heart rate, blood pressure, and blood sugar levels to increase and the blood vessels to constrict, preparing the body to meet stressful challenges

serotonin a hormone and a neurotransmitter that help transmit messages between cells, stimulate smooth muscles, and regulate learning, sleep and mood; found in the brain, blood, serum, and mucus membrane of the stomach

Types of Mental Illness		
Category	**Major Characteristic**	**Specific Illnesses**
ANXIETY DISORDERS	EXCESSIVE WORRY OR FEAR	GENERALIZED ANXIETY DISORDER, PANIC DISORDER, PHOBIAS, OBSESSIVE-COMPULSIVE DISORDER, POSTTRAUMATIC STRESS DISORDER
MOOD DISORDERS	PROLONGED UPS AND DOWNS, OR JUST DOWNS, IN MOOD	MAJOR DEPRESSION, DYSTHYMIA, BIPOLAR DISORDER, SEASONAL AFFECTIVE DISORDER, POSTPARTUM DEPRESSION
DISSOCIATIVE DISORDERS	MENTAL SEPARATION FROM STRESSFUL EVENTS	DISSOCIATIVE AMNESIA, DISSOCIATIVE IDENTITY DISORDER, DEPERSONALIZATION DISORDER
EATING DISORDERS	ABNORMAL AND UNHEALTHY EATING PATTERNS	ANOREXIA NERVOSA, BULIMIA NERVOSA
PERSONALITY DISORDERS	RIGID AND UNHEALTHY WAYS OF COPING WITH LIFE	OBSESSIVE-COMPULSIVE, DEPENDENT, AVOIDANT, HISTRIONIC, NARCISSISTIC, BORDERLINE, PARANOID, SCHIZOID, SCHIZOTYPAL, PASSIVE-AGGRESSIVE, AND ANTISOCIAL PERSONALITY DISORDERS
SLEEP DISORDERS	ABNORMAL AND DISRUPTIVE SLEEP PATTERNS	INSOMNIA, HYPERSOMNIA, NARCOLEPSY, SLEEP APNEA, PARASOMNIA
SOMATOFORM DISORDERS	PHYSICAL ACHES AND PAINS WITHOUT A MEDICAL CAUSE	SOMATIZATION DISORDER, CONVERSION DISORDER, HYPOCHONDRIASIS, CHRONIC PAIN DISORDER
DEMENTIA	LOSS OF MEMORY AND OTHER MENTAL FUNCTIONS	ALZHEIMER'S DISEASE, AIDS, STROKE, BRAIN TUMOR
PSYCHOSES	LOSS OF TOUCH WITH REALITY	STROKE, BRAIN TUMOR, DELUSIONAL DISORDER, SCHIZOPHRENIA

Defense Mechanisms. Defense mechanisms are unhealthy ways of coping with emotional pain. They include **denial**, which is refusing to see a difficult situation as it really is, and **repression**, which is burying a painful memory or emotion. These and other defense mechanisms are unhealthy because they mask problems rather than solve them. Although defense mechanisms can temporarily help people get through difficult times, they do not aid them in coming to terms with their emotional pain.

Help for Mental Health Problems. Getting help for mental health problems may prevent them from developing into more serious mental illnesses. Sources of help include SOCIAL SUPPORT SYSTEMS, SUPPORT GROUPS, PSYCHOTHERAPY, DRUG THERAPY, and ALTERNATIVE MEDICINE.

MORE SOURCES See www.mentalhelp.net

MENTAL ILLNESS A general term for disorders that involve disturbances in thinking, emotions, or behavior. The boundary between MENTAL HEALTH and mental illness is not a clear-cut line. Most people have occasions when they feel "down in the dumps," anxious, or panicky. Such feelings are normal from time to time. However, if the feelings persist and cause serious distress or interfere with the ability to function in daily activities, they are likely to be symptoms of more serious mental illness.

Epidemiology. Mental illness can strike males and females and children as well as adults. People from every racial, ethnic, educational, and socioeconomic group can develop mental illness.

Causes of Mental Illness. Mental illness is caused by a combination of several factors. In most cases the underlying biological cause is abnormal levels of brain chemicals, such as **serotonin**, that help transmit messages between brain cells. The biological abnormalities often appear to be genetically controlled and inherited. Nonetheless, even identical twins, who have exactly the same genes, have only a 50-percent chance of developing the same mental illness. This is because other factors—including the stresses and losses experienced throughout life and the support received from family and friends—can make people either more or less likely to develop a mental illness.

Types of Mental Illness. Mental illnesses can be classified into several major categories, as shown in the table on page 64. Doctors use strict guidelines to diagnose specific mental illnesses within each category.

Costs of Mental Illness. Mental illness can be as debilitating as heart disease or cancer. Some of the most disabling mental illnesses are BIPOLAR DISORDER, PANIC DISORDER, SCHIZOPHRENIA, and DEPRESSION. Because depression is so common, it is the leading cause of disability among adults in the United States. The financial burden of mental illness is also enormous. Loss of worker productivity, payments for disability insurance, and the costs of diagnosing and treating mental illness total more than $100 billion each year.

Mental illness contributes to physical illness as well. For example, people who are chronically depressed may have less resistance

---

VICTIMS OF MENTAL ILLNESS
At any given time 40 million Americans suffer from mental illness. Half of all Americans will have a mental illness at some time in their lives.

Rates of Mental Illness among Children and Adolescents in the U.S.	
	Best estimate **(%)
Any Anxiety Disorder	16.4
SIMPLE PHOBIA	8.3
SOCIAL PHOBIA	2.0
AGORAPHOBIA	4.9
GAD	3.4
PANIC DISORDER	1.6
OCD	2.4
PTSD	3.6
Any Mood Disorder	7.1
MD EPISODE	6.5
UNIPOLAR MD	5.3
DYSTHYMIA	1.6
BIPOLAR I	1.1
BIPOLAR II	0.6
SCHIZOPHRENIA	1.3
NONAFFECTIVE PSYCHOSIS	0.2
SOMATIZATION	0.2
ASP	2.1
ANOREXIA NERVOSA	0.1
SEVERE CONGITIVE IMPAIRMENT	1.2
Any Disorder	21.0

[Source: U.S. Surgeon General, *Mental Health: A Report of the Surgeon General,p* 1999.]

to infections such as colds and flu. Mental illness can even be fatal. It is the most frequent cause of SUICIDE, and it can lead to risky behaviors, such as reckless driving or intravenous drug use, that may result in death.

About 5 percent of children and teens are severely disabled by mental illness. In young people mental illness can lead to failure at school, use of alcohol or other drugs, violent behavior, and suicide.

Social and Legal Issues. Before its biological basis was understood, mental illness was often seen as an indication of moral weakness, and the mentally ill were looked down on. Many people still tend to think this way and hold mentally ill people responsible for their own illnesses. This is unreasonable and unfair, and it may lead to discrimination against the mentally ill.

An important legal issue relating to mental illness is the question of whether people who are mentally ill should be forced to receive treatment against their will. Since the 1980s many states have passed laws forcing mentally ill people into treatment. Supporters of the laws argue that mentally ill people may be too confused or irrational to get the treatment they need. Other people believe that this is a violation of their civil rights.

Risk Factors. For most mental illnesses, having a close relative with the disorder increases one's chances of developing it. Experiencing stressful life events, such as changing schools or having a parent diagnosed with a serious disease, can also increase the chances of developing most mental illnesses, especially in people who are genetically susceptible.

Treatment. The majority of mental illnesses can be effectively treated with PSYCHOTHERAPY, DRUG THERAPY, or a combination of the two. SOCIAL SUPPORT SYSTEMS, SUPPORT GROUPS, and a wide variety of ALTERNATIVE MEDICINE treatments can also help people with mental illness. Accurate and early diagnosis is the key to successful treatment. With early treatment the patient's response tends to be faster and more complete, and there are usually fewer relapses, or recurrences of symptoms. Unfortunately, about three-fourths of people with mental illness do not receive any treatment at all or get only inadequate treatment.

Preventing Relapses. Relapses of many mental illnesses can usually be prevented or at least reduced in number and severity. Abuse of substances such as alcohol and other drugs is the single most common cause of relapses, so avoiding such substances is important. Keeping regular hours, avoiding too many obligations and commitments, and continuing to take the medications prescribed for the illness can also help reduce relapses. [*See also* LAWS AND MENTAL ILLNESS; MENTAL HEALTH PROBLEMS; MENTAL ILLNESS AND CRIME.]

MORE SOURCES See www.drkoop.com

MENTAL ILLNESS AND CRIME About 5 percent of mentally ill people exhibit violent behavior or commit crimes. Only a few mental illnesses, including some PERSONALITY DISORDERS, actually increase the chances of violent or criminal behavior, however. Instead, most of the crimes committed by the mentally ill—such as vagrancy, petty theft, and public intoxication—are not due to mental illness per se but to the circumstances in which many mentally ill people live.

Often mentally ill people either discontinue treatment or cannot afford it. Without treatment people with serious mental illnesses such as SCHIZOPHRENIA may be so disabled that they are unable to support or care for themselves. The most seriously ill often become homeless. In fact, mentally ill people make up about one-third of all homeless people in the United States. Many people who are seriously mentally ill also abuse alcohol or other drugs. It is these conditions, and not any criminal tendencies associated with mental illness itself, that lead to many of the crimes committed by the mentally ill. [See also ADDICTION AND MENTAL HEALTH; DRUG ABUSE AND MENTAL HEALTH; LAWS AND MENTAL ILLNESS; VIOLENCE AND MENTAL HEALTH.]

MOOD DISORDERS Mental illnesses characterized by abnormal mood swings. Mood disorders fall into two categories—unipolar disorders and BIPOLAR DISORDER. Together they are among the most common and debilitating of all mental illnesses. Both types of mood disorders are associated with a high risk of SUICIDE.

Unipolar Disorders. Unipolar disorders are more common than bipolar disorder. They are characterized by periods of depressed mood. Specific unipolar disorders include major DEPRESSION, dysthymia, SEASONAL AFFECTIVE DISORDER (SAD), and POSTPARTUM DEPRESSION. Major depression and dysthymia are the most common unipolar disorders. Together, they affect at least 10 percent of the population. They are twice as common in females as males.

Top Ten Causes of Disablity, Worldwide 1990s	Total (millions)	Percent of Total
All Causes	472.7	
1. Unipolar major depression	50.8	10.7
2. Iron deficiency anaemia	22.0	4.7
3. Falls	22.0	4.7
4. Alcohol use	15.8	3.3
5. Chronic obstructive pulmonary disease	14.7	3.1
6. Bipolar disorder	14.1	3.0
7. Congenital anomalies	13.5	2.9
8. Osteoarthritis	13.3	2.8
9. Schizophrenia	12.1	2.6
10. Obsessive compulsive disorders	10.2	2.2

[Source: U.S. Surgeon General, *Mental Health: A Report of the Surgeon General,* 1999.]

Besides feeling down, people with any form of depression are likely to suffer from a sense of guilt and worthlessness. Nothing gives them pleasure, and they lose interest in life. They are also likely to withdraw from friends and family, and the social isolation tends to make their symptoms worse. In addition, people with depressed mood may lose their appetite, have difficulty sleeping, or suffer from physical aches and pains.

Bipolar Disorder. Bipolar disorder is characterized by periods of depressed mood alternating with periods of MANIA, or excessively elevated and excited mood. The periods of depression are the same as those that occur with unipolar disorders. The periods of mania are characterized by frantic activity, sleeplessness, overconfidence, and impulsiveness. Between 1 and 2 percent of the population has bipolar disorder. It is equally common in both genders.

Causes of Mood Disorders. Mood disorders are caused by abnormal levels of the brain chemicals serotonin and norepinephrine, both of which help transmit messages between brain cells. The abnormalities of brain chemistry are probably genetically controlled and inherited, explaining why mood disorders tend to run in families. Other factors are also involved, however, because many people with a strong family history of mood disorders never develop one themselves. Stressful life events and lack of support from friends and family, among other factors, may contribute to the development of mood disorders in people who are genetically at risk.

Treatment of Mood Disorders. Mood disorders are among the most treatable of all mental illnesses. DRUG THERAPY with ANTIDEPRESSANTS such as Prozac or Zoloft, often coupled with PSYCHOTHERAPY, can successfully relieve symptoms of depression in at least 80 percent of people with unipolar disorders. Bipolar disorder is more difficult to treat. It requires mood-stabilizing drugs, such as lithium or Depakote, in addition to antidepressants and psychotherapy. Mood-stabilizing drugs usually must be continued for life. [See also LAWS AND MENTAL ILLNESS.}

OBSESSIVE–COMPULSIVE DISORDER (OCD) A MENTAL

ILLNESS characterized by obsessions and compulsions. **Obsessions** are recurring disturbing thoughts or mental images. **Compulsions** are repeated ritualized behaviors. For example, fearing one has forgotten to turn off an appliance such as a stove is a common obsession. It is likely to be accompanied by a compulsion to check repeatedly—perhaps hundreds of times each day—to see if the appliance has been turned off.

Obsessive-compulsive disorder should not be confused with obsessive-compulsive personality disorder. A personality disorder is, on the one hand, a type of mental illness characterized by serious and persistent distortions in the total personality. Every perception, attitude, feeling, and behavior is affected.

Obsessive-compulsive disorder, on the other hand, is an anxiety disorder. Like other ANXIETY DISORDERS, fear is at its root—fear of a hot appliance burning down the house, for example, or fear of the body being contaminated by germs. The fear becomes an obsession and produces such ANXIETY that the person is compelled to relieve it–for instance, by washing the hands repeatedly to rid them of germs. Sooner or later, the ritual that helps bring the anxiety temporarily under control comes to control the person who performs it.

Epidemiology. Obsessive-compulsive disorder is a relatively common mental illness, occurring in about 2.5 percent of the population. It usually begins during the teens or twenties, and it occurs about as often in males as females. It appears to be caused by an abnormality in the brain chemical serotonin, which helps transmit messages between brain cells.

Impact of Obsessive-Compulsive Disorder. Obsessions and compulsions are time-consuming. They are also upsetting, and they can seriously interfere with daily life. For example, someone with obsessive-compulsive disorder might become so afraid of the germs he imagines everywhere that he can no longer leave his house.

The family members of people with obsessive-compulsive disorder suffer as well. It is painful to see a loved one tortured by repetitive, futile rituals. Sometimes family members are even dragged into the rituals. For example, they might be asked repeatedly throughout the day to check if the stove is turned off or the doors are locked.

Treatment. Obsessive-compulsive disorder can be treated effectively with ANTIDEPRESSANTS, which correct the serotonin abnormality in the brain, and with PSYCHOTHERAPY. The most effective type of psychotherapy for obsessive-compulsive disorder

Keywords

compulsions repeated ritualized behaviors
obsessions recurring disturbing thoughts or mental images
panic attack sudden feeling of terror accompanied by physical sensations of extreme fear

is BEHAVIORAL THERAPY. It can help by desensitizing the patient to the feared object or situation. For example, someone with an obsession about germs might be asked to practice handling dirt and then not washing his hands for increasing lengths of time. With repeated exposure to the anxiety-provoking object or situation without performing the compulsion, usually the anxiety lessens, and the compulsion weakens its hold.

ORGANIC BRAIN DISORDERS See DEMENTIA.

OVERDOSE AND SUICIDE See SUICIDE.

PANIC DISORDER An ANXIETY DISORDER characterized by repeated panic attacks. A **panic attack** is a sudden feeling of sheer terror, accompanied by all the physical sensations of extreme fear—racing heart, profuse sweating, trembling, trouble breathing, nausea, dizziness. People having a panic attack often feel as though they are going to die. Their symptoms typically peak in about 10 minutes and subside within an hour.

Panic attacks can occur in any anxiety disorder, but in other anxiety disorders they occur only in response to particular objects or situations. In panic disorder, on the other hand, the attacks occur for no apparent reason. This unpredictability causes people with panic disorder great ANXIETY about when and where the next attack will occur. They may become so afraid of having a panic attack that they develop a PHOBIA, called **agoraphobia,** in which they fear and avoid places where they have had panic attacks in the past. Eventually, they may become afraid of so many places that they never leave home. People with panic disorder also have a high risk of SUICIDE.

Epidemiology. Panic disorder occurs in about 1 percent of the population. It usually begins in the late teens or twenties. The disorder tends to run in families.

Causes of Panic Attacks. There are two different theories about why panic attacks occur; both may be valid. One notion is that panic attacks occur because the body too readily produces **adrenaline,** which is the hormone that prepares the organs for "fight-or-flight" in dangerous situations. The least little scare, according to this theory, can trigger the production of adrenaline in some

Keywords

adrenaline hormone that stimulates the heart and other organs to prepare a person for fighting or fleeing from danger
agoraphobia a strong and irrational fear of open or public spaces; agoraphobics typically choose to remain in their own homes, only leaving if they can be escorted by someone they trust
paranoia irrational belief that others are out to harm you, a feature of some mental illnesses

Panic attacks may occur with no advance warning.

people and set off a panic attack.

The other idea is that panic attacks occur when people are overly concerned about bodily sensations. Every time their heart races, for example, they think they must be having a heart attack. This causes them great anxiety, and they start to hyperventilate, or breathe quickly and shallowly. Hyperventilation, in turn, causes symptoms of dizziness, faintness, and difficulty breathing. A vicious cycle is set in motion, and within minutes a full-fledged panic attack is underway.

Treatment. Panic disorder can be controlled in about 80–90 percent of people through DRUG THERAPY and PSYCHOTHERAPY. Antianxiety drugs usually control acute panic symptoms, and ANTIDEPRESSANTS can often prevent future panic attacks.

The types of psychotherapy that work best for panic disorder are COGNITIVE THERAPY and BEHAVIORAL THERAPY. In cognitive therapy the patient learns new ways of thinking to prevent panic attacks. For example, the therapist might have the patient run up and down stairs to experience a racing heart and rapid breathing in order to get used to these body sensations without panicking. In behavioral therapy the patient learns how to control the physical sensations of panic. For example, the patient might learn how to counteract hyperventilation by breathing slowly with the diaphragm.

RELAXATION THERAPY can also help people with panic disorder control their physical responses to anxiety. Specific relaxation methods include MEDITATION, HYPNOSIS, and biofeedback.

PEER RELATIONSHIPS AND MENTAL HEALTH See
SUPPORT GROUPS; SOCIAL SUPPORT SYSTEMS.

PERSONALITY The unique pattern of attitudes, thoughts, feelings, and behaviors that characterize each individual. Personality determines whether someone is shy or outgoing, quiet or talkative. It shapes whether a person tends to play down problems or exaggerate them, and whether someone usually relies on others for help or tries to solve problems alone.

Personality is partly inherited and partly the result of life experiences, especially those in early childhood. As a result, personality tends to remain relatively stable throughout life. For example, shy children usually grow up to be quiet, reserved adults.

Personality influences how people respond to virtually everything that happens to them throughout life. It therefore plays an enormous role in how their lives turn out. It also plays an important role in their MENTAL HEALTH.

PERSONALITY DISORDERS Mental illnesses characterized by serious and persistent personality problems. PERSONALITY is the unique pattern of attitudes, thoughts, and behaviors that make up each individual. People with personality disorders tend to have unrealistic perceptions of themselves and others, unhealthy emotional responses, and abnormal ways of interacting with other people. For example, some people with personality disorders are distrustful of everyone and treat everyone with suspicion. Others feel so shy and inadequate in social situations that they live in isolation.

Doctors diagnose each specific personality disorder based on strict criteria, but an individual can have traits of more than one of

Personality Disorders	
Disorder	**Outstanding Trait**
Obsessive-Compulsive	Needs to be perfect and in control
Dependent	Depends on others for everything
Avoidant	Feels shy and inadequate in social situations
Histrionic	Needs to be the center of attention
Narcissistic	Has an inflated self-image
Borderline	Keeps changing in mood and self-image
Paranoid	Is always suspicious of other people
Antisocial	Behaves recklessly and without regard for others
Schizoid	Dislikes any type of contact with other people
Schizotypal	Thinks and behaves strangely

these conditions. For example, people with schizotypal personality disorder often suffer from **paranoia** as well, which is a symptom of paranoid personality disorder.

Specific Personality Disorders. Ten distinct personality disorders are listed in the chart on page 73.

Epidemiology. Personality disorders most often begin by adolescence or early adulthood and typically last for life. Some, including schizoid and narcissistic personality disorders, appear to affect both sexes equally. Others seem to be more common in one sex than the other. For example, borderline personality disorder is apparently more common in women, and paranoid personality disorder appears to be more common in men.

Most personality disorders are caused by a combination of genetics and the environment. Regardless of genetic background, however, people who are seriously abused in childhood are more likely to develop personality disorders.

Consequences of Personality Disorders. Personality disorders affect every aspect of life. People with these disorders have a hard time fitting in and adjusting to new situations, and they are often difficult to get along with. They also tend to rely on DEFENSE MECHANISMS instead of more mature ways of coping with problems. Many have rocky or ruined careers and relationships. Not surprisingly, people with personality disorders have a high risk of ANXIETY, DEPRESSION, and addiction to substances. They may be at high risk of SUICIDE as well.

Treatment. Because personality filters all of a person's perceptions, people with personality disorders often do not realize they are mentally ill. Instead, they blame their problems on other people. Many receive treatment only because family members or friends urge them to get help. PSYCHOTHERAPY is usually the treatment of choice. It may help people with personality disorders see their problems more objectively and change their destructive personality traits.

Changing personality traits is very difficult, however. It may be more realistic for some people with personality disorders to learn to live with their problems rather than try to eliminate them entirely. For example, people with schizoid personality disorder, who dislike being around other people, may be able to lessen the effect of the disorder on their lives by choosing careers in which they can work alone.

SUPPORT GROUPS may also help people with personality disorders by providing support and understanding. In some cases DRUG THERAPY may be useful in controlling related problems such as depression or anxiety. In general, however, medications are not as much help in treating personality disorders as they are in treating most other types of MENTAL ILLNESS. [*See also* ADDICTION AND MENTAL HEALTH.]

PHOBIAS Mental illnesses characterized by excessive fear of certain situations or objects. Fear is a normal reaction to danger that can help keep people safe from harm. However, if fear is out of proportion to the danger, causes needless anxiety, or limits normal activities, it is no longer helpful. Such fear is likely to be a symptom of a phobia. Phobias are the most common kind of ANXIETY DISORDERS.

Types of Phobias. There are more than 200 named phobias, ranging from acrophobia, or fear of heights, to ZOOPHOBIA, or fear of animals. There is even a fear of phobias, called *phobophobia.* However, phobias can be grouped into just three basic types: agoraphobia, social phobia, and specific phobia.

Agoraphobia. Agoraphobia is the fear and avoidance of situations in which one has previously experienced a panic attack. A *panic attack* is a sudden feeling of terror, accompanied by physical sensations of extreme fear. Panic attacks occur commonly in people who suffer from ANXIETY.

Agoraphobia usually develops gradually. Someone who experiences a panic attack while riding a bus, for example, may develop a fear of buses and avoid riding them in the future to try to prevent another panic attack. Despite such precautions, additional panic attacks occur. Perhaps the next panic attack takes place in a

Phobias A–Z	
Acrophobia	Fear of heights
Arachnophobia	Fear of spiders
Bacillophobia	Fear of bacteria
Bibliophobia	Fear of books
Cleptophobia	Fear of stealing
Coulrophobia	Fear of clowns
Dentophobia	Fear of dentists
Dystychiphobia	Fear of accidents
Emetophobia	Fear of vomiting
Epistaxiphobia	Fear of nosebleeds
Felinophobia	Fear of cats
Francophobia	Fear of French things or culture
Gerontophobia	Fear of old people or of growing old
Glossophobia	Fear of speaking in public
Herpetophobia	Fear of reptiles, snakes
Hypsiphobia	Fear of height
Ichthyophobia	Fear of fish
Insectophobia	Fear of insects
Japanophobia	Fear of Japanese things or culture
Keraunophobia	Fear of lightning and thunder
Kynophobia	Fear of rabies
Ligyrophobia	Fear of loud noises
Lygophobia	Fear of darkness
Musophobia	Fear of mice
Mycophobia	Fear of or aversion to mushrooms
Necrophobia	Fear of dead things
Noctiphobia	Fear of the night
Ornithophobia	Fear of birds
Ostraconophobia	Fear of shellfish
Pathophobia	Fear of disease
Pyrophobia	Fear of fire
Ranidaphobia	Fear of frogs
Rupophobia	Fear of dirt
Sinophobia	Fear of Chinese things or culture
Sociophobia	Fear of people or society
Thanatophobia	Fear of dying
Trypanophobia	Fear of injections
Uranophobia	Fear of heaven
Venustraphobia	Fear of beautiful women
Verminophobia	Fear of germs
Wiccaphobia	Fear of witches or witchcraft
Xenoglossophobia	Fear of foreign languages
Xenophobia	Fear of strangers or foreigners
Zeophobia	Fear of jealousy
Zoophobia	Fear of animals

supermarket, so supermarkets are avoided as well. As more panic attacks occur, the number of places and situations that are feared and avoided increases. Places without an easy exit, such as airplanes and crowded theaters, are especially problematic, because the feeling of being trapped tends to make panic attacks worse. Eventually people with agoraphobia may become virtual prisoners in their own homes.

Social Phobia. Social phobia is the paralyzing fear of doing something embarrassing in front of other people. It leads to avoidance of social situations. For some people the fear is limited to specific types of situations, such as performing in a recital or giving a report in class. For other people any type of interaction with others causes anxiety. Such people are painfully shy and tend to live their lives in isolation.

Specific Phobia. Specific phobia is an irrational fear of a particular type of object or situation, such as snakes, spiders, or heights. Many people with specific phobias can trace their fear to an incident in which the object or situation first frightened them. For example, someone who was bitten by a dog as a child may develop a phobia of dogs. However, not everyone who receives a bad scare develops a phobia. People who are naturally shy, inhibited, or fearful seem to be more likely to develop phobias than others.

Treatment. Most people with phobias, especially those with specific ones, can be helped with BEHAVIORAL THERAPY. Usually, the therapist exposes the patient to increasingly frightening objects or situations until they no longer cause anxiety. For example, someone with a phobia of dogs might first be shown pictures of dogs while being encouraged to remain calm until the pictures no longer cause anxiety. Then the person might be confronted with a dog on a leash until this, too, no longer cause anxiety. Finally, the person might be encouraged to pet a dog while remaining calm.

People with agoraphobia or social phobia may also be helped by DRUG THERAPY. Antianxiety drugs such as Xanax can quell immediate feelings of anxiety. ANTIDEPRESSANTS such as Zoloft can reduce the risk of future panic attacks. [See also PANIC DISORDER.]

POSTPARTUM DEPRESSION A type of DEPRESSION that occurs in some women shortly after giving birth. About one in ten women develops a seriously depressed mood and other symptoms of depression within the first several months after childbirth. Women with a history of depression or other MOOD DISORDERS are especially at risk of developing postpartum depression.

Without treatment postpartum depression can continue for months. The symptoms may get worse and interfere with the mother's ability to care for her baby. In severe cases the mother

What about the "Baby Blues"?

Not everybody who feels depressed after giving birth suffers from postpartum depression. In fact, within a few days of childbirth at least half of all women experience a brief period of depressed mood. They feel sad for no apparent reason and cry easily. Referred to as "postpartum blues" or "baby blues," this is a normal reaction to changing hormone levels in the mother following childbirth. Typically, the blues fade in a week or two.

may even attempt SUICIDE. In most cases postpartum depression can be treated effectively with ANTIDEPRESSANTS. Some women find PSYCHOTHERAPY helpful as well.

POSTTRAUMATIC-STRESS DISORDER An ANXIETY DISORDER caused by experiencing a horrifying event. Living through rape, war, natural disaster, or other terrifying events may cause great ANXIETY. This is especially likely if the event caused feelings of helplessness. Nonetheless, most people get over such events in a matter of weeks. However, some people continue to suffer anxiety because of their experience for months or even years. These people may have *posttraumatic-stress disorder*, or PTSD.

Epidemiology. PTSD can start at any age, and in some people it lasts for life. People who already have a history of MENTAL HEALTH PROBLEMS or MENTAL ILLNESS are more likely to develop PTSD than other people. The more directly involved someone was in a traumatic event, the greater the risk of PTSD developing. For example, being tortured as a prisoner of war in Vietnam is more likely to have led to PTSD than just fighting in the Vietnam War.

Symptoms. People with PTSD keep reexperiencing the terrible event that caused their disorder. They are haunted by memories of it and have repeated nightmares about it. Many people with PTSD have flashbacks in which they vividly relive the event in their mind. Many times the memories, nightmares, and flashbacks are set off by an object or situation that reminds them of what happened. For example, a person who was nearly killed in a house fire might have flashbacks of the searing flames and choking smoke whenever a fire truck goes by.

Reexperiencing the event in these ways causes people with PTSD great anxiety. They feel jumpy and have a hard time sleeping. They may not be able to concentrate, and they tend to get angry easily. Often people with PTSD become emotionally numb and feel cut off from other people. Many also suffer from DEPRESSION.

Some people start experiencing the symptoms of PTSD soon after the horrible event occurs. Other people do not develop symptoms for months or even years after. For example, a teen who seems fine after nearly being hit in a drive-by shooting may start having PTSD symptoms six months later, when she hears a car backfire, and it reminds her of her brush with death.

Treatment. BEHAVIORAL THERAPY can often help people with PTSD. The therapist may confront the patient with reminders of the traumatic event while guiding the patient in using relaxation techniques to manage the anxiety that results. DRUG THERAPY with ANTIDEPRESSANTS such as Prozac can also help many people

A trusting relationship with a psychiatrist can help many people overcome mental health problems.

with PTSD whether or not they are depressed. [*See also* RELAXATION THERAPY.]

PSYCHIATRIST A medical doctor with advanced training in the treatment of MENTAL HEALTH PROBLEMS and MENTAL ILLNESS. Psychiatrists often specialize in particular areas of mental health, such as addiction or adolescence. Treatments used by psychiatrists include DRUG THERAPY and various forms of PSYCHOTHERAPY, such as COGNITIVE THERAPY.

PSYCHOLOGIST A mental-health professional with an advanced degree in psychology. *Psychology* is the science of mind and behavior, and a psychologist usually holds a Ph.D. in the field. Psychologists often specialize in particular types of therapy, such as FAMILY THERAPY or MARITAL THERAPY. They treat their patients with various forms of PSYCHOTHERAPY, such as BEHAVIORAL THERAPY. Some psychologists also use HYPNOSIS. However, because they are not medical doctors, in most states psychologists cannot prescribe drugs for their patients.

PSYCHOSIS Loss of contact with reality. People with psychosis cannot distinguish fact from fantasy. Psychosis is not a MENTAL ILLNESS but a group of symptoms that can occur for a variety of reasons.

Symptoms of Psychosis. Symptoms of psychosis include delusions and hallucinations, disorganized thoughts, catatonia, and lack of emotions. People with psychosis can have one or more of these symptoms.

Delusions and Hallucinations. **Delusions** are false beliefs. For example, many psychotic people believe that someone is out to get them. Other people with psychosis think that they are famous historical figures, such as Napoleon or Joan of Arc.

Hallucinations are false perceptions. Hallucinations can affect any of the five senses. For example, people with visual hallucinations see things that are not there, and people with auditory hallucinations hear sounds that are not real.

Disorganized Thoughts. The thinking of people with psychosis is jumbled and illogical. This is reflected in their speech. They tend to jump from one subject to another. They may also may make up nonsense words or repeat the same words over and over in a meaningless way.

Catatonia. Catatonia refers to bizarre body movements. Some people with psychosis sit immobile for hours. Others race around in frantic, pointless activity until they drop from exhaustion.

Lack of Emotions. People with psychosis feel few emotions and fail to find pleasure in anything. They do not respond normally to things that make other people feel happy or sad, and their faces often appear expressionless. They also tend to withdraw from other people.

Causes of Psychosis. Psychosis can be caused by abuse of drugs, including alcohol, or by physical illnesses such as stroke. In addition, people who suffer from DEPRESSION may experience psychotic symptoms if their disorder is severe. Sometimes psychosis is caused by extreme STRESS. For example, someone who walks away from a serious car crash may later start hallucinating the sounds of the crash. When psychotic symptoms occur because of stress, they often disappear within a few weeks.

The most common and serious cause of psychosis is SCHIZO-PHRENIA, a mental illness that occurs because of abnormalities in the structure and chemistry of the brain. Among other differences, the brains of people with schizophrenia have less tissue and more **dopamine**, a chemical that helps transmit messages between brain cells. The abnormalities probably do not cause psychotic symptoms directly, but they may make people more vulnerable to developing the symptoms in times of stress. For example, a teen with typical brain abnormalities may start having psychotic symptoms for the first time after experiencing the stress of losing a parent in a car crash.

Treatment. Treatment of psychosis depends on its cause. If it stems from drugs or an underlying illness, then withdrawing the drugs or treating the illness usually puts an end to the psychotic symptoms. If it comes from extreme stress in an otherwise healthy individual, a supportive environment and short-term DRUG THERA-PY with an antipsychotic drug such as Haldol usually lead to a complete cure. If psychosis entails schizophrenia, lifelong drug therapy with antipsychotic drugs, often coupled with PSYCHOTHERAPY, is usually needed to keep psychotic symptoms under control.

PSYCHOTHERAPY
Treatment of MENTAL HEALTH PROBLEMS and MENTAL ILLNESS through interactions with a mental-health professional called a psychotherapist. Psychotherapists help patients identify, understand, and change the thought processes, emotions, and behaviors that are causing them problems.

Types of Psychotherapists. Several different types of mental-health professionals practice psychotherapy. A psychotherapist may be a PSYCHIATRIST, a PSYCHOLOGIST, or a nurse or social worker with special training in psychotherapy. Often, clergy and school counselors have some training in psychotherapy.

Schools of Psychotherapy. There are a number of different schools of, or approaches to, psychotherapy. These include psychodynamic therapy, COGNITIVE THERAPY, and BEHAVIORAL THERAPY. Many psychotherapists use a combination of approaches, depending on the particular patient and problem.

Psychodynamic Therapy. This school of psychotherapy is based on the work of the famous neurologist Sigmund Freud, who believed that unconscious conflicts, often arising in childhood, underlie many mental health problems. For example, children who are neglected by their parents may grow up to be distrusting of other people and have a difficult time developing close relationships as adults. Using psychodynamic therapy, the psychotherapist tries to help the patient identify such conflicts and understand how they contribute to present problems. This is done through intensive conversations between patient and psychotherapist. Dynamic psychotherapy can be used for almost any type of mental health problem or mental illness.

Cognitive Therapy. With cognitive therapy the psychotherapist tries to help patients change distorted ways of thinking. It is based on the assumption that distorted thoughts causing people to be unhappy can be changed. For example, a person with an eating disorder might think that eating a single piece of cake will make her gain weight. The psychotherapist guides the patient in adopting more realistic and positive ways of thinking. In addition to EATING DISORDERS cognitive therapy is commonly used to treat DEPRESSION and ANXIETY DISORDERS.

Behavioral Therapy. Behavioral therapy focuses on helping patients change the outward behavioral symptoms of mental health problems and illnesses. It is based on the premise that people can replace negative behaviors with more positive behaviors if they are given reinforcement. For example, a teen who is trying to overcome his extreme shyness might reward himself with a new CD each time he attends a social function and talks with at least three different people. Behavioral therapy is widely used to treat many different mental health problems and mental illnesses, including PHOBIAS and depression.

Individual and Group Psychotherapy. Psychotherapy can involve individuals or groups. Individual therapy involves one-on-one sessions between a single patient and psychotherapist. GROUP THERAPY involves several people who have the same mental health problem or mental illness, such as addiction or depression, meeting together with a psychotherapist.

HEALTH UPDATE

Interpersonal Psychotherapy
This type of psychotherapy is not really new. It was first developed in the 1960s to treat DEPRESSION. However, it is now being used to treat many other mental illnesses, including eating disorders. Interpersonal psychotherapy focuses on difficulties in the patient's current relationships with other people. The underlying premise is that people's relationships with others affect how they feel and that how they feel affects their relationships with others. For example, a teen who is repeatedly criticized by her boyfriend may develop low self-esteem and depression. A psychotherapist using interpersonal psychotherapy would try to help her see how the relationship is adversely affecting her view of herself and her mood.

For many people group therapy is more effective than individual therapy. It takes pressure off individual patients because they are part of a group. Group members may also be able to help each other by providing moral support and advice on coping with their shared problem.

The most common form of group therapy is FAMILY THERAPY, in which family members meet together with the psychotherapist. Family therapy is especially useful when a patient's family relationships contribute to his or her problem or when other family members need help coping with the problem. For example, people with BIPOLAR DISORDER have wild mood swings and can be very difficult to live with. Family therapy can help family members understand and cope with the illness.

Effectiveness of Psychotherapy. Psychotherapy can be very effective in treating mild to moderate mental health problems and mental illness, especially when they are not causing great distress or risk of suicide. Often, however, DRUG THERAPY is also needed. Some illnesses, such as SCHIZOPHRENIA and bipolar disorder, almost always require drug therapy. Nonetheless, in these cases psychotherapy is still important to help the patient learn to cope with the illness and encourage the patient to continue with drug therapy.

The supportive relationship of the psychotherapist is part of the reason that any type of psychotherapy works. The more the patient likes, trusts, and feels comfortable with the psychotherapist, the more effective psychotherapy is likely to be.

MORE SOURCES See www.onlinepsychservices.com

RELAXATION THERAPY Treatment that helps people learn how to relax when they are stressed. STRESS itself is not a MENTAL ILLNESS, but it can contribute to mental illnesses such as ANXIETY DISORDERS and DEPRESSION. Because stress causes physiological changes, such as increased heart rate and muscle tension, it can also cause physical health problems ranging from headaches to hives. Continued stress can even depress the immune system and make people more vulnerable to infections and other illnesses.

Yoga is an alternative method of relieving stress.

A number of different relaxation methods can reverse the physiological changes associated with stress and bring about a state of relaxation. One method is *aerobic exercise* (see Volume 4), such as biking, swimming, or jogging. Other methods, described below, include progressive muscle relaxation, autogenic training, biofeedback, MEDITATION, and HYPNOSIS. These methods not only result in a state of relaxation after each session, they also teach people to be more aware of how their bodies respond to stress. This helps them control their physical responses to stress in the future. Biofeedback and hypnosis can be learned from a psychotherapist. The other methods can be learned through books, videos, or classes. People should choose the method that works best for them.

Progressive Muscle Relaxation. In progressive muscle relaxation people learn to relax their muscles one at a time. First, they tense a particular muscle and hold the tension for several seconds until the muscle starts to feel slightly uncomfortable. Then they slowly release the tension. This process is repeated until they have relaxed all the major muscles in their body.

Autogenic Training. The word *autogenic* means "self-originating." To use this technique, people learn how to give themselves suggestions that lead to relaxation. For example, they might imagine their arms and legs feeling so tired and heavy that they are sinking into a mattress or chair, or they might pretend they are floating on water and being gently rocked by the waves.

Biofeedback. In biofeedback people try to relax—for example, by breathing deeply and letting go of muscle tension—while monitoring their heart rate or other physical indicators of stress with a machine. With repeated biofeedback from the machine they learn how to lower their heart rate and bring about the other physical changes that occur with relaxation. Eventually they are able to control their physical responses to stress without using the machine to monitor the changes.

Meditation. To meditate, people typically sit in a quiet, comfortable place where there are no distractions and focus on an object to help them shut out other thoughts or emotions, especially stressful ones. This usually continues for at least 15 minutes and is repeated daily. In a type of meditation called *transcendental meditation* people repeat and focus on a special word as they meditate. In *yoga* (see Volume 4), another form of meditation, people hold certain positions, or postures, while they meditate.

Hypnosis. HYPNOSIS is a sleeplike state induced by suggestions from a therapist. For example, the therapist might suggest that the patient is getting very relaxed and sleepy. Once the patient is hypnotized, the therapist might make further suggestions about relaxing and staying relaxed. For example, the therapist may have the patient imagine relaxing in a hammock on a lazy summer day and tell him or her that the feeling of relaxation will continue until their next session. To be successfully hypnotized, the person must be able to concentrate and trust the therapist. People can also learn to hypnotize themselves through self-suggestions and help themselves relax whenever they feel overwhelmed by stress. [See also STRESS MANAGEMENT.]

SCHIZOPHRENIA

SCHIZOPHRENIA A MENTAL ILLNESS characterized by PSYCHOSIS, or loss of contact with reality. Although psychosis can have other causes, schizophrenia is the most common and serious reason for it. Untreated, schizophrenia is an extremely disabling illness with a high risk of SUICIDE.

Epidemiology. Schizophrenia affects about 1 percent of the U.S. population, or about 2 million people in this country alone. It strikes males and females in equal numbers. Schizophrenia typically begins in the teens or 20s, but it sometimes first appears in the 30s. After age 40, however, new cases of schizophrenia are almost unheard of.

The specific cause of schizophrenia is not known. A tendency to develop schizophrenia appears to be inherited because the illness runs in families, so it is probably genetically controlled. The brains of people with schizophrenia are also known to be abnormal in a number of ways. For example, they have an excess of dopamine, a chemical that helps transmit messages between brain cells. They also have less tissue overall, larger cavities, and reduced activity in the frontal lobe. In people who have these brain abnormalities, STRESS may contribute to the development of the disorder.

Symptoms. Many people with schizophrenia have delusions, or false beliefs. For example, they might believe that aliens are trying to kidnap them. Many also have hallucinations, that is, they see or hear things that are not really there.

People with schizophrenia are often emotionless. They rarely feel pleasure and are likely to withdraw from other people. Their thoughts are also disorganized, and their speech is jumbled and

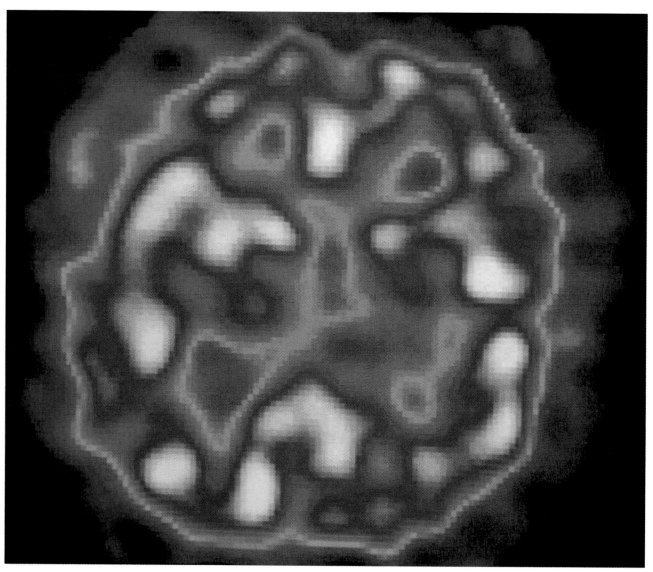

Position emission tomography allows doctors to analyze brain activity. This PET scan of a patient's brain shows the asymmetrical patterns of schizophrenia.

hard to follow. In catatonic schizophrenia they may have bizarre movements, decreased reaction to the environment, or rigidity. For example, they may rock back and forth continuously or stand motionless in odd positions for hours.

Impact of Schizophrenia. Schizophrenia can have a devastating effect on the lives of people with the illness and also on their families. The delusions, hallucinations, and other psychotic symptoms usually prevent them from attending school or holding a job. The symptoms may even prevent them from bathing, dressing, and feeding themselves. The emotional detachment makes it hard for many people with schizophrenia to maintain relationships with family and friends. Many people with schizophrenia also abuse alcohol, cocaine, or other drugs in an effort to counter the symptoms of the disease or the medications used to treat it. Drug abuse can make the illness even worse.

Treatment. Schizophrenia cannot be cured, but it can often be controlled with treatment. The earlier treatment begins, the better the outcome is likely to be. Treatment usually must be continued lifelong.

DRUG THERAPY with antipsychotic drugs can usually control the symptoms of schizophrenia by blocking excess dopamine. Although the medications have unpleasant side effects, such as **tremors**, restlessness, and weight gain, most patients must continue taking them for years to reduce relapses. Managing stress, avoiding alcohol and other drugs, and living in a supportive environment can also help control the disorder. In addition, PSYCHOTHERAPY can help patients and their families cope with both the illness and its treatment. [See also DRUG ABUSE AND MENTAL HEALTH.]

SCHOOL VIOLENCE See VIOLENCE AND MENTAL HEALTH; Volume 5.

SEASONAL AFFECTIVE DISORDER (SAD) A MOOD DISORDER in which the short days of winter bring on DEPRESSION.
Seasonal affective disorder strikes about 10 million Americans each year. It is more common at extreme northern and southern latitudes, where winter days are shorter and nights are longer. It typically begins in teens or young adults and is more common in females.

The symptoms of seasonal affective disorder include feelings of sadness, excessive sleeping, headaches, and crying spells. In the United States the symptoms usually begin in November or December, are at their worst in January, and start to improve in February. By spring the depression lifts, and it does not return again until the next fall.

Some people seem to outgrow seasonal affective disorder, while other people have it for life. There is no cure for the disorder, but it can be treated. The best treatment usually is light therapy, in which the patient sits in bright artificial light for several hours a day during the winter. Most people show significant improvement after just a few days of this treatment.

SELF-HELP GROUPS See SUPPORT GROUPS.

SLEEP DISORDERS Conditions characterized by abnormal patterns of sleep or abnormal behaviors during sleep. Most people have problems sleeping on occasion. People with sleep disorders have sleep problems severe enough to interfere with their ability to function. Specific sleep disorders include insomnia, hypersomnia, narcolepsy, sleep apnea, and parasomnia.

Insomnia. Insomnia is difficulty falling or staying asleep. It causes people to be sleepy during the day. Insomnia is the most common sleep disorder, affecting about 25 million Americans.

Causes. Insomnia has many different causes. STRESS, abuse of substances such as caffeine or alcohol, and use of some medications, including decongestants, can all cause insomnia. Certain medical problems, including *Alzheimer's disease* (see Volume 8), can also interfere with sleep, as can any illness that causes pain, coughing, or itching. In addition, some mental illnesses, including DEPRESSION and ANXIETY DISORDERS, may cause insomnia.

For many people with insomnia poor sleep habits are the cause. Eating a large meal or exercising before bed, keeping irregular hours, and taking daytime naps are some of the habits that can contribute to poor sleep. They interfere with the body growing sleepy at normal bedtime hours or being tired enough to sleep through the night.

Impact of Insomnia. Too little sleep can cause irritability and poor concentration and coordination. Being sleepy while operating a motor vehicle or other machinery, for example, can lead to accidents because of increased reaction time and the tendency to nod off. Lack of sleep can also aggravate the symptoms of some mental illnesses, including DEPRESSION and BIPOLAR DISORDER. Extreme lack of sleep can even cause hallucinations and other symptoms of PSYCHOSIS.

Treatment. Treatment of insomnia depends on its cause. If stress, drug use, or illness is the cause, then managing stress, avoiding the drug, or treating the illness usually cures the insomnia. If poor sleep habits are the cause, sleep may be improved by going to bed and getting up at the same time each day, avoiding daytime naps, and doing something relaxing, like taking a warm bath, before bed. Sleep medications such as sedatives should be used only for a short time, if at all, because they are addictive and become less effective the longer they are used.

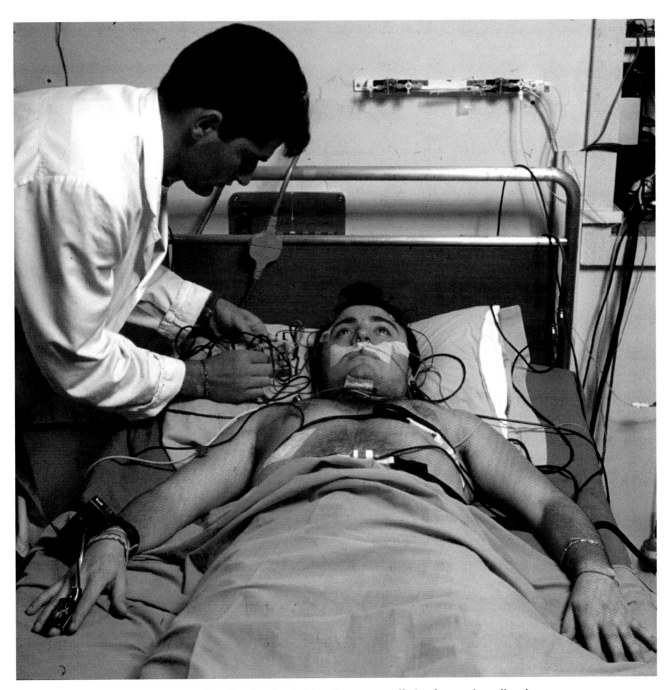

A specially trained therapist may monitor the sleeping habits of a person suffering from a sleep disorder.

Other Sleep Disorders. Other sleep disorders are less common than insomnia. However, they may be equally disruptive of daily life.

Hypersomnia. Hypersomnia is excessive sleep. People with hypersomnia sleep more at night than most people but wake up feeling groggy and unrested. Hypersomnia has many of the same causes as insomnia, and treatment depends on the cause.

Narcolepsy. Narcolepsy is characterized by repeated daytime sleep attacks. People with this disorder can nod off at any time, even in the middle of a conversation or at the wheel of their car. They start yawning uncontrollably and within seconds or minutes fall fast asleep. If left undisturbed, they are likely to sleep soundly for half an hour or so and then wake up feeling refreshed, only to nod off again within a few hours. Narcolepsy is caused by an inherited nervous system abnormality. It can be treated with stimulant drugs that help prevent daytime sleepiness.

Sleep Apnea. In sleep apnea periods of loud snoring alternate with periods in which breathing stops for up to half a minute at a time. The loud snoring interrupts sleep and causes daytime drowsiness not only for people with the disorder but for their partners as well. Obesity is a common cause of sleep apnea, and weight loss often corrects the problem.

Parasomnia. Parasomnia is characterized by abnormal sleep behaviors. In *nightmare disorder*, for example, people are repeatedly awakened from sleep by recurrent, terrifying dreams. The dreams may be so frightening that they cannot go back to sleep, or they try to avoid falling asleep in order to prevent the nightmares from occurring. In *sleepwalking disorder* people get out of bed, walk around and do simple tasks, all the while staring blankly ahead. Brain-wave patterns of sleepwalkers indicate that they are in state more similar to waking than to sleeping and dreaming. Nonetheless they seem unaware of their surroundings, and if awakened while sleepwalking they are confused and disoriented.

The cause of parasomnia is not known, although stress or drug use may trigger the behaviors. There is no specific treatment. Parasomnia is most common in children, who usually outgrow it by adolescence. When parasomnia persists past childhood, it may be a sign of underlying MENTAL HEALTH PROBLEMS and MENTAL ILLNESS.

SOCIAL SUPPORT SYSTEMS Networks of family members, friends, and other trusted people who can provide help and encouragement in times of STRESS. Everyone needs a circle of people to care for, accept, and emotionally support them. With supportive people around them they are more likely to bounce back from disappointment and loss. Without such support they are at greater risk of developing MENTAL HEALTH PROBLEMS and MENTAL ILLNESS.

Maintaining a Strong Social Support System. Having supportive friends and relatives does not just happen. It takes work. In order to have people to rely on in times of stress, one must be there for other people when they are in need. Keeping in touch and staying involved with others when times are good is important as well.

Unfortunately, people with mental illness often withdraw from others. If they suffer from DEPRESSION, for example, they may find no pleasure in life and avoid social activities. Some people with mental illness can also be hard to get along with because of their symptoms. For example, if they have PERSONALITY DISORDERS, such as paranoid personality disorder or narcissistic personality disorder, they may be suspicious and paranoid or vain and self-centered. For these reasons people with mental illness may have to work especially hard to maintain social support systems.

Support Groups. Not everyone is fortunate enough to have a circle of supportive family members and friends. However, they need not feel alone. SUPPORT GROUPS can at least partly fill the gap. There are support groups for people with mental health problems such as ANXIETY or low self-esteem, for people facing life crises such as death or divorce, and for people with mental illnesses such as depression or PHOBIAS. Support group members can provide moral support, practical advice, and hope to other members of the group. Support groups for specific problems can be found in the classified section of newspapers and on the Internet.

SOMATOFORM DISORDERS Mental illnesses in which emotional problems are expressed as physical symptoms. Most people occasionally experience physical symptoms such as headaches or nausea when they are under STRESS. However, people with somatoform disorders have stress-related physical symptoms that are so severe, long lasting, or upsetting that they interfere with daily life.

Epidemiology. Somatoform disorders typically begin in adolescence or young adulthood. They often recur throughout life. The disorders tend to occur more often in females than males.

Somatoform disorders usually first occur as a reaction to severe emotional stress. People who are most likely to respond this way are those who have other mental illnesses, including PERSONALITY

DISORDERS, ANXIETY DISORDERS, or DEPRESSION. People who have close relatives with somatoform disorders are also more likely to develop them, suggesting they may be caused in part genetically.

Specific Somatoform Disorders. Specific somatoform disorders include somatization disorder, conversion disorder, and hypochondriasis.

Somatization Disorder. People with somatization disorder have a history of many different unexplained physical symptoms. Typical symptoms include headaches, nausea, and diarrhea. The symptoms tend to worsen during times of emotional stress.

Conversion Disorder. In conversion disorder emotional problems are turned into nervous-system problems. Common symptoms include paralysis, double vision, or deafness. The symptoms almost always occur when a person is facing a crisis or dealing with a particularly stressful situation.

Hypochondriasis. People with hypochondriasis assume that every physical symptom is an indication of serious medical illness. For example, if they have a headache, they think they must have brain cancer. They remain convinced that they are seriously ill even after repeated assurances by doctors that they are fine.

Treatment. Before treatment of a somatoform disorder begins, the possibility of an underlying physical illness must be ruled out. Treatment is difficult and not always successful, because most people with somatoform disorders do not believe that their physical symptoms are due to psychological causes. With these disorders it is especially important for patients to have a good relationship with a medical doctor who can help relieve their physical symptoms and also reassure them that they are being taken seriously.

Treatment usually includes PSYCHOTHERAPY, which aims at resolving the emotional problems underlying the physical symptoms. Sometimes HYPNOSIS is used to help identify the underlying emotional problems. RELAXATION THERAPY can help many patients cope with the stress that triggers their disorder. Some patients also improve with ANTIDEPRESSANTS, especially if depression is contributing to their illness.

STRESS Tension that affects both mind and body. Stress is an unavoidable part of every person's life. Major disruptions, such as moving to a new house or changing schools, can be very stressful. However, minor annoyances, such as oversleeping or losing a library book, can cause some amount of stress. Stress can even occur as a result of positive events, such as being selected for a role in a play.

Teens and Stress. The teen years can be especially stressful. Adolescence is a time of rapid biological and emotional change, and becoming sexually mature causes many teens stress, particularly when raging hormones lead to unpredictable mood swings. Maturation usually brings new responsibilities and commitments that can also add to the stress. It can also be stressful to separate from parents and establish an individual identity. In addition to these typical stresses of adolescence, today's teens face tensions that were less common just a couple of generations ago. Many teens now witness violence, for example, or lose a parent through divorce.

The Impact of Stress. A little stress can actually improve one's performance. For example, someone who is feeling tense because of an upcoming recital may be motivated by it to practice more and be better prepared. However, too much stress can cause both physical and MENTAL HEALTH PROBLEMS. Even if stress does not cause health problems, it can lower the quality of life.

Stress and Mental Health. Stress can be a direct cause of MENTAL ILLNESS. For example, ADJUSTMENT DISORDER occurs when people react to stress in a way that is more extreme or disruptive than normal. A teen with adjustment disorder might be so distraught after not getting the lead in a play, for example, that she contemplates SUICIDE. POSTTRAUMATIC-STRESS DISORDER is another mental illness that stems from stressful events, such as rape, war, or natural disasters.

Stress can also be a contributing factor in many other mental illnesses. It can trigger or aggravate symptoms in people with DEPRESSION, BIPOLAR DISORDER, ANXIETY DISORDERS, SOMATOFORM DISORDERS, DISSOCIATIVE DISORDERS, and SCHIZOPHRENIA.

How Stress Affects Individuals. The way particular people are affected by stress depends on a number of factors. One factor is PERSONALITY, which in turn is a product of genetics and the environment. Because of differences in personality some people always bounce back no matter how many stressful events they experience, while others fall apart as soon as the going gets rough.

Another factor that determines how stress affects individuals is whether they have SOCIAL SUPPORT SYSTEMS. Having a circle of understanding, supportive friends and family members can go a

HEALTH UPDATE

The Effects of Stress
Recent research proves what many people already know from personal experience: Stress can make people sick. Scientists have shown that too much stress can suppress the immune system and make people more susceptible to infections such as colds. It can also lead to the immune system overreacting, and it can cause allergies and asthma. In addition, it can contribute to the development of heart disease and other serious medical conditions.

Stress Scale For Teens

Stress	Event Values
1. Death of Spouse, Parent, Boyfriend/Girlfriend	100
2. Divorce (of yourself or your parents)	65
3. Puberty	65
4. Pregnancy (or causing pregnancy)	65
5. Marital Separation or Breakup with Boyfriend/Girlfriend	60
6. Jail Term or Probation	60
7. Death of Other Family Member (other than spouse, parent, or boyfriend/girlfriend)	60
8. Broken Engagement	55
9. Engagement	50
10. Serious Personal Injury or Illness	45
11. Marriage	45
12. Entering College or Beginning Next Level of School (starting junior high or high school)	45
13. Change in Independence or Responsibility	45
14. Any Drug or Alcohol Use	45
15. Fired at Work or Expelled from School	45
16. Change in Alcohol or Drug Use	45
17. Reconciliation with Mate, Family, or Boyfriend/Girlfriend (getting back together)	40
18. Trouble at School	40
19. Serious Health Problem of a Family Member	40
20. Working While Attending School	35
21. Working More Than 40 Hours per Week	35
22. Changing Course of Study	35
23. Change in Frequency of Dating	35
24. Sexual Adjustment Problems (confusion of sexual identify)	35
25. Gain of New Family Member (new baby born or parent remarries)	35
26. Change in Work Responsibilities	35
27. Change in Financial State	30
28. Death of a Close Friend (not a family member)	30
29. Change to a Different Kind of Work	30
30. Change in Number of Arguments with Mate, Family, or Friends	30
31. Sleep Less Than 8 Hours per Night	25
32. Trouble with In-Laws or Boyfriend's or Girlfriend's Family	25
33. Outstanding Personal Achievement (awards, grades, etc.)	25
34. Mate or Parents Start or Stop Working	20
35. Begin or End School	20
36. Change in Living Conditions (visitors in the home, remodeling house, change in roommates)	20
37. Change in Personal Habits (start or stop a habit like smoking or dieting)	20
38. Chronic Allergies	20
39. Trouble with the Boss	20
40. Change in Work Hours	15
41. Change in Residence	15
42. Change to a New School (other than graduation)	10
43. Presently in Premenstrual Period	15
44. Change in Religious Activity	15
45. Going in Debt (you or your family)	10
46. Change in Frequency of Family Gatherings	10
47. Vacation	10
48. Presently in Winter Holiday Season	10
49. Minor Violation of the Law	5

[Source: *Journal of Psychosomatic Research*, 1967.]

long way in helping people cope with stress. How stress affects individuals also depends on the number and severity of stressful events they experience in life. People who experience a series of several stressful events are likely to be more affected by stress than those who experience just one or two.

Stressful Events. Any major change in a person's life, whether it is good or bad, can be stressful. Some events are more stressful than others. The chart on page 94 lists stressful events that many adolescents experience. They are ranked according to how stressful they are for most teens, with the most stressful events listed first. The stress level is compounded when more than one stressful event is experienced simultaneously or within a short period of time.

Coping with Stress. Everyone has to cope with stress at least once in awhile. Some people choose ways of coping that are unhealthy. For example, they may rely on DEFENSE MECHANISMS, such as **denial**, which is refusing to see a difficult situation as it really is.

Another unhealthy way some people cope with stress is by abusing substances such as alcohol or other drugs. Substance abuse may temporarily help people forget their problems. However, the problems are likely to still be there after the effects of the substance wear off. In addition, substance abuse itself usually creates even more stress in the long run. For example, it may lead to absences from work or school, reckless behavior, broken relationships, and *addiction* (see Volume 1).

Stress Management. Healthy ways of coping with stress include learning how to manage it. The first step in managing stress is to record all the events and situations that cause stress. This helps identify the main sources of stress.

Learning specific STRESS MANAGEMENT techniques, such as prioritizing, may eliminate some of these sources of stress. For example, a teen might choose to go out for a team or to get a job after school but not to do both, which would put him under too much stress. Other sources of stress may at least be reduced if not eliminated. One way to reduce stress is to try to view problems as challenges rather than obstacles. For example, an upcoming exam may be less stressful if it is seen as motivation to master the material rather than as a chance to fail. In addition, considering problems one at a time can also make them seem less stressful.

Other Healthy Ways of Coping. When stress cannot be eliminated or reduced, it takes less of a physical and mental toll on people who are physically and emotionally healthy. Therefore maintaining good health is another way to cope with stress. Supportive friends and family members may also help people resist the adverse effects of stress by providing them with positive feedback and encouragement. People who feel overwhelmed by stress may benefit from PSYCHOTHERAPY. A type of psychotherapy called RELAXATION THERAPY can teach people how to relax when they are feeling stressed out. Specific relaxation techniques include MEDITATION and HYPNOSIS. [See also ALCOHOL AND MENTAL HEALTH; DRUG ABUSE AND MENTAL HEALTH; STRESS AND THE IMMUNE SYSTEM.]

STRESS AND THE IMMUNE SYSTEM STRESS, or tension, especially when severe or long lasting, can cause negative changes in physical and MENTAL HEALTH. One way stress adversely affects physical health is through its influence on the immune system.

Hormones produced during times of stress suppress normal immune-system functioning. As a result, people under stress may be more susceptible to colds, flu, bacterial infections, and even cancer. Other hormones produced during times of stress stimulate immune cells that are involved in allergic reactions. Because of this, people under stress may develop allergy symptoms such as eczema, hives, sneezing, or itchy eyes. In addition, in people with asthma stress may lead to asthma attacks. [*See also* STRESS MANAGEMENT.]

STRESS MANAGEMENT Everyone experiences STRESS, or tension, in their life, especially teens. However, for some people stress becomes so great or is endured over such a long period of time that it contributes to physical and MENTAL HEALTH PROBLEMS, including headaches, heart disease, lowered resistance to infections, ANXIETY, sleeplessness, and DEPRESSION. Because stress can be so unhealthy, it is important to know how to manage it.

Identifying Sources of Stress. The first step in managing stress is to identify what is causing it. The best way is to keep a stress diary or record of all the events that cause stress, ranging from minor annoyances, like missing a bus, to major life changes, such as moving to a new city. A stress diary should be kept for a least a few weeks to identify stresses that occur just once in a while as well as those that occur on a regular basis.

Eliminating or Reducing Sources of Stress. Reviewing the list of events that cause stress can help people determine which sources of stress they might be able to eliminate or reduce. Common sources of day-to-day stress that are often relatively easy to eliminate include always running late, not having time to relax, and feeling overwhelmed by commitments. Learning how to say "no" when asked to take on more than one can handle, establishing priorities, and setting realistic goals can help eliminate these sources of tension. Being organized can also help by decreasing the amount of time it takes to get things done.

Other sources of stress may be impossible to eliminate, but they can still be reduced by adopting a more positive attitude. When people see their problems as challenges that will help them grow rather than as hurdles that they cannot overcome, the problems are likely to cause less stress. Considering problems one at a time instead of all at once can also make them more manageable and less stressful. In addition, taking positive steps to overcome problems rather than stewing about them can reduce the stress they cause. For example, sitting down to tackle a difficult homework assignment and working on it until it is finished is likely to cause less tension than putting off the assignment until the last minute and worrying about it in the meantime.

Resisting the Effects of Stress. When causes of stress cannot be eliminated or reduced, it is still possible to resist stress's adverse physical and mental effects. One way is to stay healthy and energetic by following commonsense habits: eating according to the *Food Pyramid* (See Volume 4), getting 8–10 hours of sleep each night, and doing some kind of vigorous physical activity several times a week. Talking over problems with friends and family members and just staying involved with others can also help reduce the physical and mental toll.

Professional Help for Stress. Some people need professional help when they are feeling overwhelmed by stress. Seeking the help of a PSYCHOLOGIST or PSYCHIATRIST when stress is too great to handle is a good investment in one's physical and MENTAL HEALTH. An effective form of therapy for stress is RELAXATION THERAPY, which teaches people how to relax when they are feeling stressed out. Specific relaxation techniques include MEDITATION and HYPNOSIS.

DRUG THERAPY with sedatives or tranquilizers can also help people relax when they are under stress. However, the drugs tend to become less effective the longer they are taken; they can also be addictive. Therefore drugs are at best a short-term solution for stress. [See also SOCIAL SUPPORT SYSTEMS; STRESS AND THE IMMUNE SYSTEM.]

SUICIDE The act of taking one's own life. In the United States suicide is a major public health problem, especially among teens. Prevention is the key to reducing rates of suicide and controlling its devastating effects on people's lives.

Suicidal Thoughts and Behaviors. Most people who commit suicide usually think about it for days or weeks ahead of time. The mildest suicidal thoughts are passive ones. For example, someone might wish to not wake up in the morning or to be killed in a car crash. Such thoughts may evolve to more active thinking about suicide, such as considering ways to take one's own life. Suicidal thoughts may progress to suicidal behaviors, which include suicide gestures and SUICIDE ATTEMPTS as well as completed suicides, which actually result in death.

Suicide gestures are actions or plans that are related to suicide but are not actual attempts to take one's life. For example, a person might write a suicide note or plan how to steal a gun. Suicide attempts are actions that are intended to be fatal but are not. Someone might take ten sleeping pills, for example, instead of the 20 that would be deadly. Suicide attempts must be taken very seriously because they are often repeated and eventually may succeed.

Epidemiology. In the United States suicide is one of the top ten causes of death for people of all ages. It is the second leading cause of death among teens. In 1998, 11 out of every 100,000 Americans committed suicide. Suicide rates are higher in people without any college education. They are also higher in urban than rural areas.

Risk Factors. There are several risk factors for suicide. The most important are MENTAL ILLNESS and substance abuse.

Mental Illness and Substance Abuse. More than 90 percent of people who commit suicide have a mental illness, abuse alcohol or other drugs, or have both problems. About half are intoxicated at the time they take their lives, and the majority suffer from DEPRESSION. Other mental illnesses with a high risk of suicide include BIPOLAR DISORDER, some PERSONALITY DISORDERS, and SCHIZOPHRENIA.

Social Factors. People who have recently undergone a major loss or disappointment are especially likely to commit suicide. It could be loss of a boyfriend or girlfriend or disappointment over being cut from the basketball team. Lack of SOCIAL SUPPORT SYSTEMS can increase the risk. People without a circle of supportive

Suicide and Death Rates per 100,000				
Age	**Total Deaths**		**Per 100,000**	
	Men	**Women**	**Men**	**Women**
0–4	0	0	0.00	0.00
5–9	7	0	0.06	0.00
10–14	234	83	2.37	0.88
15–19	1,463	274	14.56	2.89
20–24	2,069	329	23.00	3.79
25–29	2,182	426	23.60	4.56
30–34	2,663	535	22.20	5.26
35–39	2,633	776	23.66	6.83
40–44	2,633	765	24.28	6.92
45–49	2,213	668	23.92	6.95
50–54	1,683	567	22.01	7.02
55–59	1,318	389	22.13	6.03
60–64	987	269	20.35	4.69
65–69	1,030	229	23.45	4.40
70–74	1,131	207	29.32	4.19
75–79	1,075	198	35.87	4.69
80–84	925	157	52.43	5.29
85+	686	165	57.77	4.37
UNKNOWN	17	0		
Total	**24,538**	**6,037**	**18.58**	**4.37**

[Source: Center for Disease Control and Prevention, 2000.]

friends and family members are more likely to commit suicide because they have no one to help them through times when they feel especially down or hopeless.

Other Risk Factors. An important risk factor for suicide is a prior suicide attempt. Living alone increases the risk because many people who live alone are socially isolated and lack social support systems. Having access to a lethal weapon is another risk factor, making it easier for people to carry out suicidal thoughts. Having a family member who committed suicide also increases the risk, in part because there is strong genetic component in mental illnesses with a high risk of suicide. Older people who have fatal diseases or diseases that are very painful or disabling are also at greater risk of suicide than people who are in good health.

Suicide: Cost to the Nation

- EVERY 17 MINUTES ANOTHER LIFE IS LOST TO SUICIDE. EVERY DAY 86 AMERICANS TAKE THEIR OWN LIFE AND OVER 1500 ATTEMPT SUICIDE.
- SUICIDE IS NOW THE EIGHTH LEADING CAUSE OF DEATH IN AMERICANS.
- FOR EVERY TWO VICTIMS OF HOMICIDE IN THE U.S. THERE ARE THREE DEATHS FROM SUICIDE.
- THERE ARE NOW TWICE AS MANY DEATHS DUE TO SUICIDE THAN DUE TO HIV/AIDS.
- BETWEEN 1952 AND 1995, THE INCIDENCE OF SUICIDE AMONG ADOLESCENTS AND YOUNG ADULTS NEARLY TRIPLED.
- IN THE MONTH PRIOR TO THEIR SUICIDE, 75% OF ELDERLY PERSONS HAD VISITED A PHYSICIAN.
- OVER HALF OF ALL SUICIDES OCCUR IN ADULT MEN, AGES 25-65
- MANY WHO MAKE SUICIDE ATTEMPTS NEVER SEEK PROFESSIONAL CARE IMMEDIATELY AFTER THE ATTEMPT.
- MALES ARE FOUR TIMES MORE LIKELY TO DIE FROM SUICIDE THAN ARE FEMALES.
- MORE TEENAGERS AND YOUNG ADULTS DIE FROM SUICIDE THAN FROM CANCER, HEART DISEASE, AIDS, BIRTH DEFECTS, STROKE, PNEUMONIA AND INFLUENZA, AND CHRONIC LUNG DISEASE COMBINED.
- SUICIDE TAKES THE LIVES OF MORE THAN 30,000 AMERICANS EVERY YEAR.

[Source: Surgeon General, *The Surgeon General's Call to Action to Prevent Suicide*, 2001.]

Sexual Orientation and Suicide. The suicide rate among gays and lesbians has consistently been higher than among the heterosexual population. Recent studies have also shown that homosexual students are four times as likely to attempt suicide as heterosexual students. Some experts have noted that homophobia is a health hazard that leaves lifelong emotional scars on victims.

In 2001 the American Medical Association (AMA) proposed a resolution asking national youth groups to not exclude gays. AMA members believe that such exclusionary policies could drive young people to suicide. They noted that rules that do not ban gays would help "lower the increased risk of suicide in the adolescent population." Supporting this claim are other studies that show teen suicide rates are lower in states that have antidiscrimination laws.

Suicide Methods. The most common method of attempted suicide is drug overdose. The most common method of completed suicide, at least in the United States, is gunshot. It is used primarily by males and explains why they have higher rates of completed suicide than females. Hanging is another method used primarily by males. Females are more likely to use less violent methods that are also more likely to fail, including poisoning, drug overdose, and drowning.

The Impact of Suicide. Many people who attempt or commit suicide feel their friends and family would be better off if they were dead. The reality is far different. The suicide of a loved one can have devastating effects on the survivors, and it is likely to haunt them for the rest of their lives.

The friends and family members of people who commit suicide are often left with tremendous feelings of guilt and remorse. They may torment themselves that they should have seen the suicide coming and done something differently to prevent it. For religious or moral reasons some people believe that committing suicide is sinful or shameful. Because of this attitude the survivors of a suicide may feel ashamed of what happened and try to cover it up by telling other people that the death was accidental. This can cause the survivors even more suffering and prevent them from coming to terms with the suicide. In some cases the survivors feel angry at the deceased for causing them so much emotional pain.

Warning Signs of Suicide. Although it is not always possible to know when someone is thinking about suicide, most of the time there are warning signs. Often people who are contemplating suicide talk about it before they attempt it. Other SUICIDE WARNING SIGNS include sadness, loss of interest in normal activities, and feelings of worthlessness. Preoccupation with death, withdrawal from social interactions, and giving away personal belongings are also common in people who are thinking about taking their own life.

Help for Suicidal Thoughts and Behaviors. People considering suicide need immediate help. If you are thinking about suicide, you should call a suicide hotline, such as the National Suicide Hotline at 1-888-248-2587. If someone you know is talking about suicide or shows other warning signs, urge the person to get help, and tell a responsible adult. If someone has already attempted suicide, call 911.

Prevention. Getting help for any mental illness or substance abuse problem is usually the best way to prevent suicide. DRUG THERAPY and PSYCHOTHERAPY can help ease the dark moods of depression and the symptoms of many other mental illnesses as well as help

Fact or Folklore?

Folklore Talking about suicidal thoughts will make them worse.

Some people are afraid to ask loved ones if they are thinking about suicide. They fear that they will plant suicidal thoughts that may not already be there or that talking about suicidal thoughts will make them worse. In fact, just the opposite is likely to happen. Asking people about suicidal thoughts gives them a chance to share their feelings and you a chance to show them you care.

people recover from substance abuse, thus eliminating the two most significant risk factors for suicide. Other ways to help prevent suicide include maintaining good mental health—for example, by working to build a positive self-image—and keeping involved with family and friends. [See also ADDICTION AND MENTAL HEALTH; ALCOHOL AND MENTAL HEALTH; DRUG ABUSE AND MENTAL HEALTH; SUICIDE HOTLINES.]

SUICIDE ATTEMPTS Actions intended to lead to SUICIDE that are not fatal. Some people who attempt suicide survive because they use methods that do not work. For example, a person might cut his wrist but not deeply enough to cause a fatal loss of blood. Other people who attempt suicide survive because they are discovered in time to be saved. For example, someone might jump off a bridge and be rescued by a passerby.

Females, especially adolescent females, attempt suicide more often than males. However, males are more likely to die by their own hand. This is because females generally use methods such as drug overdose or poisoning that are less likely to kill than the more violent methods, including gunshots and hanging, that males typically use.

Suicide attempts must be taken very seriously. People who try to kill themselves should be evaluated and treated by a mental health professional, such as a PSYCHOLOGIST or PSYCHIATRIST. They may need to be hospitalized for a few days to ensure that they do not attempt suicide again as well as to treat any self-inflicted injuries. Without treatment another attempt is likely, and the next time it might succeed. [See also SUICIDE HOTLINES; SUICIDE WARNING SIGNS.]

SUICIDE HOTLINES Toll-free 24-hour telephone or Internet services offering help for people who are suicidal. Suicide hotlines are operated by suicide-prevention centers around the country. Their mission is to help prevent SUICIDE in people who are having suicidal thoughts and behaviors.

Suicide hotline calls or messages are answered by specially trained volunteers. They try to establish a relationship with the people who contact them. Volunteers may offer advice for dealing with problems and remind those they are talking to that they have friends and family members who love them. If someone has already committed a suicidal act, such as taking a drug overdose, volunteers try to locate the individual and send help.

Several national suicide hotline numbers are listed in the Directory of Services, Organizations, and Hotlines at the back of this book. Local numbers can be found in the yellow pages under suicide prevention.

MORE SOURCES See www.suicidehotlines.com

SUICIDE WARNING SIGNS Behaviors and other signs that indicate someone may be at risk of SUICIDE. Some suicides occur without any prior clues. However, most are preceded by warning signs.

Because the majority of people who commit suicide suffer from DEPRESSION, signs and symptoms of depression are also potential warning signs of suicide. For example, people who are at risk of suicide may feel sad most of the time and take no pleasure in things they once enjoyed. They may also lose their appetite and have a hard time sleeping.

Another suicide warning sign is a preoccupation with suicide and death. For example, someone contemplating suicide might repeatedly watch a movie or read a book in which a character commits suicide. Practicing risky behaviors, such as abusing alcohol or driving recklessly, may be a warning sign as well. People at risk of suicide may also give away their favorite possessions, write a will, buy a gun, or hoard pills. Others may make veiled suicide threats, such as, "You'd be better off if I were dead!"

People who exhibit warning signs of suicide need immediate help. People who show these signs should be urged to contact a suicide hotline or to see a mental health professional as soon as possible. A responsible adult should also be informed. The sooner suicidal people get help, the sooner they are likely to feel better and be out of danger. [See also SUICIDE HOTLINES.]

SUPPORT GROUPS Organizations that provide support for people with particular problems. There are support groups for people dealing with virtually any type of problem, including MENTAL HEALTH PROBLEMS such as low self-esteem, life crises such as divorce, MENTAL ILLNESS such as DEPRESSION, or addictions such as *alcoholism* (see Volume 1).

Types of Support Groups. Some support groups are advocacy groups, mainly providing information about problems and how to get help for them. Other support groups are self-help groups, in which people with a particular problem meet regularly and give each other encouragement and advice. Some support groups are both advocacy and self-help groups. Most support groups have national toll-free numbers, Web sites, and e-mail addresses to contact for assistance. There are many support groups devoted to special types of mental illness and mental health needs. For example, there are special support groups for anxiety, depression, GRIEF, and self-esteem issues.

Advocacy Groups. Advocacy groups provide detailed, up-to-date information about a problem, such as its causes, risk factors, and rates of occurrence. They also usually have information on treatment resources across the country and the latest treatment options. In addition, many advocacy groups work to heighten public awareness of the problem and to fight for the rights of people with the problem. Examples of advocacy groups are the National Eating Disorders Organization, National Foundation for Depressive Illness, National Alliance for the Mentally Ill, and Anxiety Disorders Association of America.

Self-Help Groups. Self-help groups provide members with acceptance, moral support, and practical advice on coping with their mutual problem. For many people simply sharing their concerns and experiences with others who have the same problem is extremely helpful. Many national self-help groups have local meetings all over the country. The best-known self-help group is Alcoholics Anonymous. Others include Narcotics Anonymous, Gamblers Anonymous, and Obsessive-Compulsive Anonymous.

Alcoholics Anonymous. Alcoholics Anonymous, or AA, deserves special mention. It was the first successful self-help group, and many other self-help groups are modeled on it. AA has helped more people recover from alcoholism than any other treatment approach. Every day more people around the world attend AA meetings than receive any other form of treatment.

At AA meetings members give each other advice, encouragement, and acceptance as they struggle to remain alcohol-free. The meetings also provide members with an opportunity to socialize without alcohol. In addition to the help they receive at meetings, AA members can contact other members whenever they need help abstaining from alcohol. The 12-step program of Alcoholics Anonymous has been adopted by other many other self-help groups, including Gamblers Anonymous and Obsessive-Compulsive Anonymous. It is based on the personal experience of the founding members of AA and serves as a guide to new members as they struggle to abstain from alcohol for life. [See also

ALCOHOL AND MENTAL HEALTH; SOCIAL SUPPORT SYSTEMS.]

MORE SOURCES See www.alcoholics-anonymous.org; www.psychcentral.com

TEENS AND MENTAL HEALTH See AIDS AND MENTAL HEALTH; ALCOHOL AND MENTAL HEALTH; EATING DISORDERS; MENTAL HEALTH; SLEEP DISORDERS; STRESS; SUPPORT GROUPS.

TIC DISORDERS Conditions characterized by frequent tics—involuntary, repetitive movements or vocalizations that occur rapidly and suddenly. Examples of tics include eye blinking and throat clearing. People with tic disorders cannot resist the urge to perform the tics, and afterward they have a sense of released tension. Tics usually occur in bouts throughout the day. They may occur nearly every day or only sporadically.

Causes. The primary cause of tic disorders is thought to be an abnormality in brain chemicals, such as **dopamine**, that help transmit messages between brain cells. Tics often get worse when people are under STRESS, so stress may also contribute to development of the disorders.

Types of Tic Disorders. There are two types of tic disorders: simple tic disorder and Tourette's disorder. Simple tic disorder involves just one or two obvious gestures or sounds, such as shoulder shrugging or grunting. It usually begins in childhood and often is outgrown by adolescence or adulthood.

Tourette's disorder is more serious. It typically involves both movements and vocalizations. The tics are also likely to be complex. For example, a person with Tourette's disorder might repeatedly perform a series of movements such as stomping, bending, and knee jerking, and also keep repeating the final phrases that other people say. People with Tourette's disorder often develop low self-esteem because other people ridicule their strange behavior, not realizing it is unintentional. Tourette's disorder usually begins in childhood and lasts for life. It is more common in males than females.

Treatment. People with simple tic disorder may not need treatment unless the movements or vocalizations are disruptive or cause embarrassment and low self-esteem. More serious cases, especially cases of Tourette's syndrome, can be treated by a PSYCHIATRIST with DRUG THERAPY or BEHAVIORAL THERAPY. The drugs that are most effective can have harmful side effects, so they are reserved for the most serious cases. Behavioral therapy often involves a technique called *habit reversal training*, in which people are taught to counter an urge to tic by making the opposite movement—for example, lowering the shoulder to counter an urge to shrug. SUPPORT GROUPS, such as the Tourette Syndrome Association, can also help people with tic disorders by providing information, treatment sources, and other support.

TOURETTE'S DISORDER See TIC DISORDERS.

VIOLENCE AND MENTAL HEALTH There is more violence in the world today than in previous generations, and teens are the most common victims of violence. Almost half of teens know another teen who has been shot. Being a victim of violence can have a negative effect on MENTAL HEALTH and can sometimes cause MENTAL ILLNESS. On the other hand, being mentally ill does not necessarily lead to violent behavior, which is a common misconception.

How Violence Affects Its Victims. Victims of violence are likely to experience stressful feelings of helplessness and fear. They commonly develop ANXIETY DISORDERS and DEPRESSION. In cases of life-threatening violence, such as rape or war, victims may develop POSTTRAUMATIC STRESS DISORDER. People with this disorder keep reliving the violence in dreams and other mental images, which causes great ANXIETY. Victims of severe childhood abuse may develop an anxiety disorder called *dissociative identity disorder*. They evolve one or more separate personalities to deal with incidents of violence and other abuse that are too great for them to handle any other way.

Mental Illness and Violent Behavior. Occasionally someone with a severe untreated MENTAL ILLNESS commits a violent act that receives a great deal of media attention. For example, John Hinckley, the man who tried to kill President Ronald Reagan in 1981, was suffering from untreated SCHIZOPHRENIA at the time of the attempted assassination. Such random acts have led to the misconception that people with mental illness are prone to violence. In truth, only a few percent of mentally ill individuals ever commit violent acts. [See also ABUSE AND MENTAL HEALTH; LAWS AND MENTAL ILLNESS; MENTAL ILLNESS AND CRIME.]

X

XENOPHOBIA The fear of foreign or strange things, people, or cultures. It may include fear or hatred of people from different countries, of other races or sexual orientations, or of the disabled. Individuals or groups exhibiting xenophobia—called *xenophobes*—often attempt to isolate the "foreign" people. For example, they may seek to pass laws attempting to keep foreigners out of the country, or they may violently attack the people or objects they fear. Xenophobia and racism are often combated through education programs.

Z

ZOOPHOBIA The fear of animals. Living one's life attempting to avoid the feared animal or animals may severely restrict one's life and cause a great deal of social suffering. Treatment often includes behavior therapy, especially *desensitization*, a process in which the patient is slowly exposed to the animal or animals causing the fear in a safe and nonthreatening situation over a period of time. In this way the fear is minimalized, and the patient is able to cope with the fear. Psychotherapy and drug therapy may also be useful in the treatment of zoophobia.

Concerns and Fears

Have you ever been afraid, only to find out there was nothing to fear after all? Every school has a scary rumor or two that goes around every year—a student went crazy from the formaldehyde fumes in the biology lab, or they put Spanish fly in the spaghetti sauce in the cafeteria. (The stories nearly always turn out to be false.) Or have you ever done something without the slightest fear, then discovered that you were actually putting your life at risk? Every year in Florida, for instance, kids on vacation swim into underwater caves and do not come out alive.

Feeling either too much fear or too little fear about a situation happens all the time. Both can make you unhappy, and both can harm you either psychologically or physically. Having an exaggerated view of risks causes exaggerated fears, which can make you feel anxious and stressed out. Feeling this way for a prolonged period can make you physically ill. Having little concern about real risks can fool you into thinking everything is fine when you are headed for trouble. The stakes are especially high when the risks or fears involve your health.

The solution is knowledge. If you picture this confusion about what is risky as a sea of trouble, then knowing the true nature of health risks is your life preserver. Not only will knowledge keep you from going under, it will put you in a better position to make healthy choices. Often you will find you can actually save yourself.

COPING WITH SOCIAL PHOBIA

The trouble with trying to tell whether or not a teen has true social phobia is this: almost every teen has at least a few of the symptoms. Teens with social phobia feel afraid in all kinds of social settings. They often:

- Feel highly sensitive to criticism
- Have trouble being assertive
- Are unhappy with themselves
- See small mistakes as enormous
- Feel that everyone is watching them
- Fear speaking in public, dating, or talking to persons in authority

Less common among all teens, but typical of some teens with social phobia, according to the National Mental Health Association (NMHA), are fear of using public restrooms or eating out, or fear of talking on the phone or writing in front of others. Social phobia is not the same as shyness. People with social phobia can be at ease with others most of the time, except in particular situations.

A *phobia* is a fear of something that poses little or no actual danger. Not only are phobias irrational, they are disabling. The extreme feelings of terror, dread, or panic can interfere with a teen's normal life. Think about it. What if you were afraid to speak to teachers or store owners? What if dropping your fork made you want to run out of the cafeteria and never come back?

Social phobia is an anxiety disorder, and a fairly common one. It usually begins in adolescence, and increasing evidence suggests that family factors may play an important role in a teen's developing this condition.

ANXIETY DISORDERS are the most common mental illnesses in America. They affect as many as one in ten young people. Having an anxiety disorder is different than having an occasional bout of "nerves"—a pounding heart on a first date or sweaty palms in the dentist's office are normal. But if fear interferes with school or work, leads you to avoid certain situations, or keeps you from enjoying life, you need to have it checked out.

See a PSYCHIATRIST or a PSYCHOLOGIST, and get treatment. Mental health professionals take phobias very seriously. And with treatment phobias can be overcome. You can learn coping skills that will help you react differently to situations that once scared you. This is one mental illness that can often be cured for good.

DEALING WITH DYSTHYMIA

You cry a lot because you feel so sad all the time. You complain about everything, feel negative, have temper tantrums. You have lost interest in people, things you used to like—everything. You forget things. You have trouble concentrating or making decisions. You feel terrible about yourself. You feel guilty. You want to sleep all the time, or you wake up often during the night and stare at the ceiling. At least one of your parents has suffered from major depression.

If at least two of these sound like you, you may have dysthymia, or dysthymic disorder. For years people with dysthymia were accused of being bad-natured. Dysthymia was classified as a character disorder; the individual's main problem was diagnosed as a depressive personality or negative temperament. The word itself means "ill humored." Today dysthymia is known to be a mood disorder like major DEPRESSION but harder to recognize because it has fewer symptoms and is more chronic—that is, it goes on and on.

Dysthymia usually begins in childhood or adolescence, according to the U.S. Surgeon General's Report *Mental Health*. Teenagers with dysthymia are depressed for most of the day, on most days, and symptoms continue for several years—usually for about 4 years. Sometimes they are depressed for so long that they do not recognize their mood as out of the ordinary; they may not complain of feeling depressed. Many are relieved to be told they have a treatable illness. About 70 percent of children and adolescents with dysthymia eventually experience an episode of major depression. Studies have shown that about 5 percent of teens experience dysthymia— that is, about one in 20.

As with more severe depression, the main risks of dysthymia come with not getting treatment. Studies show that if the disorder is allowed to go on, the untreated sufferer may lead a narrower life with fewer friends and more STRESS and may miss educational and job opportunities. Unfortunately, mental health professionals are usually consulted only when major depression develops, although dysthymia alone, allowed to go on and on, may lead to alcoholism or suicide.

The treatment picture for dysthymia, however, is positive. The new generation of ANTIDEPRESSANTS, particularly SSRIs, are proving safe and effective for treating teens' symptoms. The success of prescribed medication, according to *Scientific American*, removes the stigma associated with this mental disorder that used to be considered a personality problem.

COOLING IT WITH CHRONIC STRESS

You need *some* stress in your life, just to keep you alert. And most teens are used to handling a number of *stressors*—things that cause stress—at once. In a week you might juggle studying for a major test, playing in a sports event, keeping up with your tasks at home, developing a romance, and maybe holding down a part-time job.

But chronic stress is different. It is what people usually mean when they say they feel stressed out. You feel overwhelmed. You may feel angry, unfairly criticized, and impatient. You may worry about everything. And you often will have physical symptoms.

Chronic stress is the result of long-term problems, and these are often out of a teen's control—having a serious illness; dealing with your parents' divorce; coping with an alcoholic or drug-addicted or abusive parent. (Continually trying to do too much can also trigger chronic stress—but that is something you *can* control. See the entry on STRESS MANAGEMENT in this volume.)

Just to be clear about our terms: *Stress* is not

the pressure from the outside—the first semester of college, the SATs, the patrol car in your rearview mirror are all *stressors*. Stress is your psychological, emotional, and physical reaction to those situations.

If you have two or more of the symptoms on the following list, you may be suffering from chronic stress:

- Having an upset stomach, diarrhea, or indigestion
- Having a headache or backache
- Having trouble falling asleep
- Eating too much or too little
- Feeling hostile, angry, or irritable
- Feeling anxious
- Avoiding other people
- Crying
- Feeling frustrated with minor things

The risk of ignoring the symptoms, and ignoring your stress, is that it will get worse. Stress can make you very sick. Some medical experts believe that up to 90 percent of all illness is stress-related. Another risk comes from using substances to make yourself feel better. Popular choices for reducing or combating stress include sugar, caffeine, alcohol, drugs, and tobacco. Unfortunately, not only are these quick fixes all temporary, in fact they eventually increase stress. (If you thought you were stressed out before, imagine the stress of life as an addict or an alcoholic.)

What to do about chronic stress? None of the solutions are startling or magical, and some of them are difficult to begin—but all of them feel good. Here are four ways to work toward a less stressful you: Start getting some exercise, hang out with supportive friends, get into fun non-school activities, and learn how to put things in perspective.

The trick is to take it slow and easy. You do not need to add to your stress, for instance, by plunging into an elaborate exercise program. Start with short walks or bike rides—any exercise will help. Try meditation or yoga or martial arts or simple stretching.

Get with friends you like, and do things you like—go to a movie, go on a picnic, play putt-putt golf, go to the mall, listen to music. Get out of your house and out of your own head. Check out your school's clubs. Help Habitat for Humanity build a house. Learn to play the guitar. Try new things—anything that is not school or work or that feels hard to do.

Keep things in perspective by stepping back and letting go. If you are stressed out about some immediate event—a test, a fight with a friend—mentally take a step back from the situation. Ask yourself: How important is it when you look at your whole life? What is the worst that can happen? What would you tell a friend facing the same problem? "Letting go" works for any kind of stress, especially for things beyond your control—for instance, a friend who is drinking too much or a bad-tempered boss. Understanding and accepting that you cannot change another person can be an enormous relief. Letting go of what other people say or do or think gives you nothing but freedom.

Many schools have school psychologists or counselors who are trained to help teenagers deal with stress. All teens face difficult days, tough times, and hard choices, but no teen needs to live life overwhelmed by chronic stress.

SURVIVING SCHIZOPHRENIA

Teens with schizophrenia are split off from *reality*. Schizophrenia interferes with their ability to think clearly, manage emotions, make decisions, and relate to others. It is a lifelong disease that can be controlled but not cured. The first signs typically emerge in the teenage years or twenties.

One of the reasons schizophrenia in children and teens is often not diagnosed is that parents and teachers think the symptoms are just more of the same odd kid behaviors, maybe slightly exaggerated. Here are some of the signs specialists in adolescent schizophrenia look for, according to the American Academy of Child and Adolescent Psychiatry:

- Seeing things and hearing voices that are

not real (hallucinations)

- Unusual or bizarre thoughts and ideas
- Confusing television and dreams with reality
- Confused thinking
- Extreme moodiness
- Ideas that people are "out to get them" or talking about them
- Behaving like a younger child
- Severe anxiety and fearfulness
- Difficulty relating to peers and keeping friends
- Withdrawn and increased isolation

A lot of your friends probably exhibit at least some of these signs, and—luckily for all of us—none of them by themselves indicates that a person is mentally ill. Parents, teachers, and friends can begin to worry when they see a combination of these signs and when behaviors like these get worse over the course of weeks

Scientists still do not know the specific causes of schizophrenia, but research has shown that the brains of people with schizophrenia are different, as a group, from the brains of people without the illness. As recently as the 1980s doctors could not offer much help or hope to schizophrenics.

Today antipsychotic drugs are allowing more and more young people with schizophrenia to go to work or school full time, get married, and lead full lives. There are special programs aimed at young people who have their first psychotic episode—their first extended break with reality—between the ages of 16 and 25. Early treatment can keep them from ever having to go into a psychiatric hospital, as nearly all schizophrenics have had to in the past.

Many people with schizophrenia have written about what it is like to be lost in the illness. Each of them has struggled with unique imaginings and fears. Kristin Viana wrote a prize-winning essay published in the Fall/Winter 1993 issue of *Soundings East*. She described herself as "an eight year old asking the man in the mirror questions. His face is not her reflection; she

hopes his face is not her reflection." By the time she was thirteen, she knew there was something wrong, although no one around her did. She saw "bloated images of people she knows are still alive float over her bed at night and dribble vaseline into the air . . . . Unicorns fly by and the people in the walls call her name." Kristin celebrated her sixteenth birthday locked up in a mental institution.

At 20, Kristin was a junior in college making excellent grades. She took a lot of medication every day to keep her head clear, and she still forgot things sometimes. But she writes that she "has found company with people who are not the most popular or beautiful. She stands in alliance with people that have won."

RECOVERING FROM PTSD

Survivors of trauma show up on our TV screens every night on the news—a little boy pulled from a well, a family huddled next to their mobile home flattened by a tornado, students running from a school building with the splat of gunshots in the background, refugees wandering dazed through rubble-strewn streets. Traumatic events can happen to anyone, at anytime—a flood, hurricane, or fire; a kidnapping or rape; a car or plane crash; the suicide of a friend; sexual or physical abuse; street violence.

Just how at risk is the average teen for experiencing trauma? From the few studies available, 15–43 percent of girls and 14–43 percent of boys have experienced at least one traumatic event in their lifetime—that is, about 1–4 of every 10 young people. Of those children and adolescents who have experienced a trauma, 3–15 percent of girls and 1–6 percent of boys—fewer than 1 in 10 of them—will suffer from posttraumatic-stress disorder, or PTSD. Roughly speaking, about 1 in 100 average teens may be dealing with PTSD, according to these figures from the National Center for PTSD—which of course means that 99 out of 100 are not.

POSTTRAUMATIC-STRESS DISORDER (PTSD) is exactly what it says it is—ongoing stress suffered as a result of being exposed to trauma. Rates of

PTSD are much higher in children and adolescents who have been exposed to particularly awful trauma. For example, studies have shown that as many as 100 percent of children who see their parent killed or sexually assaulted, 90 percent of sexually abused children, 77 percent exposed to a school shooting, and 35 percent of urban youth exposed to community violence develop PTSD.

Teens who have experienced trauma and feel unable to regain control of their lives or who are experiencing the following warning signs for more than a month should talk to a counselor or mental health professional, according to the American Psychological Association:

- Recurring thoughts or nightmares about the event
- Trouble sleeping or changes in appetite
- Anxiety and fear, especially when exposed to events that remind you of the trauma
- Memory problems, including difficulty in remembering aspects of the trauma
- Inability to face certain aspects of the trauma, and avoiding activities, places, or people that remind you of the event
- A "scattered" feeling, unable to focus on studies or daily activities; difficulty making decisions
- Irritability, easily agitated, or angry and resentful
- Depression, sadness, low energy
- Emotional numbness, feeling withdrawn, disconnected, or different from others.
- Spontaneous crying, feeling a sense of despair and hopelessness
- Extreme protectiveness of, or fear for, the safety of loved ones

In addition, teens exposed to trauma may have trouble relating to friends and family members. They may start acting on impulse or become more aggressive. Their grades may fall.

Some teens recover from PTSD on their own in a few months, but for many PTSD can go on for years if they do not seek treatment. Some teens with PTSD get help as a result of treatment for another psychiatric disorder, such as major depression, substance abuse, ADHD, or another anxiety disorder such as separation anxiety.

While the great majority of teenagers, even those who experience trauma, will never have to struggle with posttraumatic-stress disorder, treatment can help those who do. They can learn that they do not have to be scared of their memories and that the world is not always unsafe.

OVERCOMING SAD

There is a reason why people retire to Florida or Arizona, why they flee south for winter vacations. Feeling a little down in the winter is normal. The difference for people with SEASONAL AFFECTIVE DISORDER (SAD) is that they feel depressed from September or October to March or April—*all* fall and winter, year after year. During the spring and summer they feel okay, or "normal." (People with SAD who live in places like Seattle, where it rains for much of the year, can feel depressed year-round.)

And why would human beings react any differently than other animals to the changing seasons? The mood and behavior of some wild creatures changes as fall moves into winter—they may sleep more (some hibernate) and move around less. Most people find they eat and sleep slightly more in winter and dislike the dark mornings and short days. For SAD sufferers, however, the symptoms are severe enough to disrupt their lives and to cause considerable distress.

SAD is classified as a kind of major depression and has many of the same symptoms. Besides depression that begins in the fall or winter, other common signs of SAD in teens include:

- Oversleeping (trouble getting out of bed, napping or fatigue in the afternoon)
- No energy, feeling too tired to cope, too tired to move
- Little interest in school or other activities
- Overeating, carbohydrate cravings, and weight gain

• Behavioral problems

Researchers at the National Institute of Mental Health believe some 10 million Americans suffer from SAD, while another 14 percent of the adult population suffer from a milder condition known as the *winter blues*. The disorder often begins in adolescence or early adulthood, and it occurs more frequently in women than in men.

What causes SAD is still not known, but the reason for it, as you may have figured out, is not getting enough sunlight. That would explain why recent studies show that SAD is more common in northern countries—the sun shines for fewer hours a day as you go farther north. (SAD is less common in northern countries where there is snow on the ground and thus a lot of reflected light.)

The cure is fairly straightforward: more light during the winter months. Teens with a mild case of SAD may only need 30 minutes out in the morning sun to keep the winter blues away, according to Mark Levy, chair of the San Francisco Foundation for Psychoanalysis. Light therapy—sitting under special bright lights—for varying periods of time also seems to help, but the symptoms usually reappear when the therapy is discontinued.

In severe cases teens with SAD may also bene-fit from antidepressant medications. "If some-body has been clinically depressed for a couple of weeks, he or she won't have the ability to go out-side and exercise," says Levy. "And if they think they should be able to and they can't, they'll only feel worse."

SAD is fairly rare among teens, and most people with the "winter blahs" do not have the disorder. But if your winter blues come back every year along with Halloween, it is a good idea to have a psychologist evaluate your symptoms.

GRIEVING AFTER SUICIDE

If a friend of yours, or your mother or father or sister or brother, has killed themselves, you know that nearly everyone who knew them got terribly depressed. One of the most important things to know is that *no one* is to blame for someone else's death. We can love people with all our hearts, we can say only the kindest words to them and do all we can for them, and they can still decide to die.

Another thing to understand is this: there is no right or wrong way to feel after someone you love has died. All the feelings you have are appropriate. One of the most common feelings is anger at the person who committed suicide— anger that they did not ask for help, that they did not talk more about how they were feeling, that they did not do *something* that would have kept them alive.

Here are some questions you might be asking and some answers to them:

• **Why didn't I know?**
Many people in emotional pain hide it. Some people who feel suicidal show no or few signs of their risk or danger. Even if you suspect someone is deeply depressed, it is hard to accept that someone you know so well might actually kill themselves.

• **Why didn't my friend tell me?**
Even your best friend might find it hard to ask for help or to admit to mental illness. Some people feel ashamed at being suicidal. Very often they are so wrapped up in their own pain that they cannot think of anyone else. This does not mean that they did not love you.

• **Why can't I get over this?**
Feeling grief after someone you love commits suicide is normal; but if it begins to interfere with your everyday life, you may need to speak with a therapist or a grief counselor about your feelings. Many schools will address the problem of a student's suicide head-on and call in special counselors to talk with students and help them deal with their feelings. If you are having difficulty dealing with a friend's or classmate's sui-cide, it is best to talk to these counselors or another adult you trust.

It Can't Happen to Me

L ike almost all teens, you have probably wondered from time to time whether you were entirely sane. You have blue days, times when your mind feels like a squirrel in a cage, days when you cannot stop obsessing about something or someone, moments when you wish you were dead. But mentally ill? You?

What would you do if mental illness suddenly became your reality? You might feel stunned, shocked. You might deny it. You might feel angry. Or you might be relieved to finally have a name for how you feel. Finally, like most teens, you would rise to the challenge. You would eventually overcome your illness or learn how to be happy and successful despite it.

What is it like to be a teenager with a mental illness? The four stories that follow should give you some idea. All feature young people who had to confront some frightening, long-lasting conditions.

ALLISON

"I was standing around with my friends after soccer practice one night," Allison recalls, "and one of them said to me, 'What's with you, Allie?'" I realized I couldn't remember the last time I'd laughed at anything. I told them I was okay, just depressed. It was months before I found out there's a difference between having a few bad days and the way I was feeling."

How *was* she feeling? "At first, just sad. Everything, little things, would make me cry, like hearing a sad song, or not being able to find something. That went on for weeks. Somewhere in there I began to wake up just about every morning at 4 o'clock, and I couldn't go back to sleep. I would lie there and think how life didn't mean anything, nothing good would ever happen in my life again, what was the point?

Several months into this major depression, Allison's grades began to drop. "I was so tired all the time, I couldn't study. I began to miss soccer practice, and I didn't even care. After school, I would just go home and lie on my bed. Usually I would cry until my parents came home from work. I didn't want them to know how I was feeling. It wasn't that I didn't think they could help. The idea of help never entered my mind."

Not asking for help is typical of people with severe depression. Even if the idea of talking to a counselor or a teacher occurs to them, they can feel too exhausted or hopeless to follow up.

Two things happened at about the same time that would start Allison on the road to recovery. She stopped eating, and her soccer coach ran into her parents at the movies. "My parents began asking me all these questions. Why wasn't I going to practice? What did I have for lunch? Was I doing drugs? Was I drinking? Why wasn't I going out? I told them the truth, which was that I wasn't drinking, I just didn't care about anything. The next day they made an appointment for me with a psychiatrist."

One of the reasons no one got overly concerned about Allison sooner was that nothing bad had happened to her that would alert anyone to look for depression. No one had died. Her parents had not gotten divorced. She was physically healthy. She was not under any special stress. "Lots of people don't realize that clinical depression can come out of nowhere," Allison says. "When you think about it, that makes sense. It's an illness. You can come down with depression, just like you can come down with a cold."

The U.S. Center for Mental Health Services says one out of eight teens is clinically depressed;

other studies set the rate as low as one in 25. Besides the kinds of feelings and behaviors Allison had, teens who are clinically depressed may also show other warning signs or symptoms—eating disorders, problems at school due to skipped classes and a lack of interest or motivation, anger or indifference that lead them to start *drinking heavily* or *taking drugs*.

Allison's psychiatrist recommended treating her clinical depression with antidepressant medication and talk therapy.

After a few weeks on an antidepressant, as the world began to look a little brighter, Allison began to see a therapist once a week to talk about how she was feeling and her life in general. "You need to be able talk to someone who doesn't make you feel embarrassed, someone who's not judging you."

After less than a month Allison was sleeping through the night. "One day I realized I hadn't cried for a week," she said. "I was actually laughing again! But I know that people who've been depressed can get depressed again. I promised my therapist that if I feel down for more than a few days, I'll call her."

PATRICK

Jim Carrey. Cher. Whoopi Goldberg. Albert Einstein. Walt Disney. John Lennon. Thomas Edison. Just like Patrick, all are people diagnosed with or presumed to have had ATTENTION DEFICIT HYPERACTIVE DISORDER (ADHD), also called attention deficit disorder (ADD). And just like Patrick, they all have been the object of a lot of attention.

But for years the only attention Patrick got was negative. Over and over, from as far back as he can remember, his teachers and parents said the same things to him:

"Pay attention!"
"That's wrong! What did I just tell you?"
"Don't interrupt!"
"Sit down!"
"Can't you stay still?"

"In the fifth grade I decided I was getting Alzheimer's," Patrick says. "I couldn't remember *anything*. I forgot my homework every other day. I was always losing one of my shoes. I would forget to bring the right books home; or if I brought them home I forgot to bring them back to school. I forgot to go home when I was supposed to. People said I was doing it to get attention—like I needed more attention!"

Patrick would call out answers and questions in class at the wrong times. "I would interrupt like crazy, even when I didn't want to. Other kids didn't do this, and it made me wonder how they knew when it was the right time to speak up, because I knew that if I didn't say what was on my mind right away, I'd forget it."

This kind of behavior he now knows is called *impulsivity*, which is simply doing or saying things without thinking about them first. It is a typical problem for many people with ADHD. Sometimes, Patrick says, "the ideas would jump into my mind so fast, it was like popcorn popping. And I didn't know which idea to say out loud first."

Like many kids with ADHD, Patrick spent a lot of time in the principal's office, beginning in elementary school. "I wasn't bad or stupid or lazy, although for a long time I thought I was all those things," he says. "I just couldn't control myself very well. Schools are places where you're supposed to sit still and be quiet, or stand in line and be quiet, or take turns and be quiet. School and I were on a collision course."

By the time Patrick was in eighth grade, his test scores showed him several grade levels behind in both math and reading. "I had never read a whole book," he said. "I couldn't concentrate, and I was a slow reader. Finally, the school counselor had me tested. It turned out I had a reading disability. It was the psychologist who gave me those tests who told my parents I might also have ADHD. A lot of tests later, it turned out I did."

Patrick and his parents learned that about five out of 100 kids have ADHD. Even though people with ADHD usually start having problems before they are seven years old, many do not find out they have it until they are adults. Boys have ADHD about nine times more often than girls, but no one knows why. In fact, the causes of ADHD have not been discovered, although research shows that it probably has to do with different levels of certain brain chemicals and that there is a genetic link, so it tends to run in families.

When ADHD is diagnosed at an early age—in elementary school, ideally—a child can usually stay in regular classes while being treated. Patrick needed a variety of treatments. He and his family went to counseling to learn more effective ways of behaving and speaking with each other. His parents decided to get him extra academic help, and he began taking a medication prescribed by his psychiatrist.

Many symptoms of ADHD persist into adulthood, and that has been the case for Patrick. At 21 he still has problems with being disorganized and impulsive and with getting along with people. "I have pretty severe mood swings," he says, "and I can't seem to get a relationship to last more than a year or so. I don't like to be in one place for long—literally. I mean, I might come and visit you and stay half an hour, then I get itchy, need to move on. I have never sat through a movie without getting up for popcorn or a drink two or three times."

What about Whoopi Goldberg and Albert Einstein? "Well," Patrick says. "I'm still young. I'm still working on it."

DAVID

It was when he was in third grade, David remembers, that he first began to need to count things. Whenever he went up or down stairs, he had to count them, and the floor had to count as number one. "I knew there were fourteen stairs from the basement to the first floor, and sixteen from the first floor to the second floor," he says, "but I had to count them every time. For years."

He developed bedtime rituals—he had to do the same things every night, and in the same order. "For instance, I had to be sure I had clean clothes, everything had to be clean from the wash and folded exactly right. I had to lay them out on my dresser in order—my socks, my underpants, my shirt, my jeans—with an equal amount of space between them. My shoes had to be right next to each other in a special place by the dresser. The shoelaces had to be untied but crossed, right over left." He had similar rules for brushing his teeth, bathing, and an equal set of rules for what he needed to do in the morning.

"I didn't really see anything wrong with it for awhile," David said. "I just knew my day wouldn't go right if I didn't do the counting, if I didn't arrange my clothes.

"My sister told me I was crazy," David says, "and I was worried that she was right. I knew other kids didn't do the things I did.

What David was suffering from, although it would be four years before he or anyone else knew it, was OBSESSIVE-COMPULSIVE DISORDER (OCD).

"By the time I was twelve, I was miserable. My parents were yelling at me all the time. I was starting to lose my friends. I had headaches. I was depressed a lot. I was staying up later and later to get all my rituals done. I tried to keep them secret from my family, but they figured it out. Actually, that turned out to be a good thing. They took me to a therapist.

"I didn't know whether to laugh out loud or cry when the therapist asked me the standard OCD screening questions," David remembers. "Like, 'Do you have to count to a certain number or do things a certain number of times? Are there things you have to do before you go to bed or at the dinner table?' I was just waiting for her to tell me I was nuts." Instead, she told him he had OCD, along with about a million other kids and teens in the United States. She also told him she had learned that people with OCD have enormous courage. "She said we have to learn to shake hands with our fears," David said. "She was right about that."

Today, at 17, David has the disorder under control, although new symptoms pop up now and then. (OCD is a chronic disorder whose cause scientists are still debating.) "In cognitive behavior therapy I learned how to boss back the OCD thoughts. My therapist also prescribed a medication that increased the serotonin levels in my brain, and I go to a support group of teens with OCD—we laugh at ourselves a lot."

What was the best thing about going for treatment? "Finding out I wasn't crazy and the OCD wasn't my fault."

SABRINA

SUICIDE is the third leading cause of death among teens in the United States. Only car accidents and homicides (murders) kill more people between the ages of 15 and 24. One of the significant signs that a person is thinking about suicide is that *they tell you they are thinking about suicide*—or about death, or about "going away." Or they say something like, "I'd be better off dead" or "I won't be a problem for you much longer" or "Nothing matters; it's no use."

Sabrina was 16 when her 17-year-old sister, Liz, was killed by a drunk driver. When Sabrina looks back at the months after the funeral, she says she felt as if she was wandering through a gray tunnel that went nowhere. "I cried every night and off and on all day. It was an effort to talk to anyone. The air felt heavy." Her friends tried to cheer her up, she said. "But I didn't want to cheer up, I didn't want to laugh, I didn't want to go to parties, I didn't want to do anything. My house was like a tomb. My parents were both grieving too, of course."

Sabrina said she began consciously to think of killing herself about a month after her sister died. She wrote in her journal then: "The only thing that makes me feel better is when I imagine being dead. Then I would stop hurting. I would be with Liz. My sister, my best friend, I miss you! I miss you every minute! You're so funny and no one knows me and loves me like you do. Everything's stupid and empty. I'm so tired. I don't care about anything, even Jon. I tried to tell him how I was feeling and he got mad. He didn't want to hear it. He'll be better off without me."

About a week later, Sabrina took all the pills in her parents' medicine cabinet. Then she called the local suicide hotline and told them what she had done. She remembers being unsure. "I thought if it didn't work for some reason, then that would be fate. If it did work, that would be fate too. They told me later they kept me on the phone until the EMTs arrived. The next thing I remember is waking up in the hospital. By then they had pumped most of the drugs out of my stomach. Somehow I felt like my sister had told me to stay on earth, that she didn't need me with her."

Sabrina had to stay at the hospital until the doctors were convinced she was no longer a danger to herself, she says. "They had a psychiatrist come and talk to me, and my parents had to sign a paper saying I would go to therapy." As for many other teens who have attempted suicide, the treatment that proved to work best for Sabrina was the same treatment prescribed for most cases of severe depression, a combination of PSYCHOTHERAPY (talk therapy) and antidepressant medication.

Sabrina later learned that her own experience was typical. Most people who try to kill themselves are depressed. Women attempt suicide more often than men, and drug overdose is the method most often used. Women are more likely than men to use nonviolent methods, such as overdosing or drowning, rather than gunshots or hanging. Teenagers are most likely to think about committing suicide as the result of some kind of trigger event. Common triggers are a parent's divorce, a breakup with a boyfriend or girlfriend, or the death of a friend or relative.

"One of the hardest things has been talking to my friends about my suicide attempt," Sabrina says. "My counselor says it's very important for me to talk about it. Of course, most of them don't want to—one friend said she felt so guilty for not helping me she couldn't stand it. But I'm lucky. I have two really good friends who let me talk their ears off."

Even though she no longer feels stuck in that gray tunnel, Sabrina knows that people who have attempted suicide once are at risk for trying it again unless they get help for their depression. "But I *am* getting help. At first I didn't want to. I felt like if I got better I was betraying my sister somehow. Now I'm trying to understand what my therapist keeps telling me—suicide is a permanent solution to a temporary problem."

Straight Talk

For some questions there is only one answer. If you ask How much does that job pay? or Where's the gym? you can count on getting the same answers no matter how many people you ask. But often the facts fly out the window when you ask a question that people have an opinion about. How can I tell if I'm depressed? or
Why do some teens shoplift when they have plenty of money?

Some people who give biased answers to teens' questions have what they think are good reasons for doing that: They think they know what is best for the teen, and the facts do not matter as much as their own experience or steering a teen in the "right" direction. Say you ask an adult what to do about stress. If the adult remembers his teen years as one long party, he may tell you you're imagining things—"Wait til you're my age, then you can complain about stress!" Not a helpful answer.

"What should I do when my friend says she's thinking about suicide?" you might ask another adult. You may be told that people who talk about killing themselves never do it, and the best thing is not to dwell on such morbid thoughts, and certainly not to talk about them—a dangerous (possibly fatal) answer designed to steer your friend in the direction the adult thinks teens' behavior should go.

Here you will find straight answers to some common teen questions related to MENTAL HEALTH, based not on biases but on the best information available—not on opinion or emotion but on fact.

HOW CAN I TELL IF I'M CLINICALLY DEPRESSED? OR IF A FRIEND IS?

One of the dangerous myths about DEPRESSION and teenagers is that teens do not suffer from real depression, they are just moody a lot. The truth is, depression is more than being moody, and it can affect people at any age. Some other myths the National Institute of Mental Health and other health organizations warn you to watch out for:

- **Myth**: Depression is something people can snap out of if they want to.
- **Fact**: Depression is a real medical illness, and it needs to be treated.
- **Myth**: Telling an adult that a friend might be depressed is betraying a trust. If someone wants help, he or she will get it.
- **Fact**: Depression saps energy and self-esteem and can interfere with a person's ability or wish to get help. It is an act of true friendship to share your concerns with an adult who can help.
- **Myth**: Talking about depression only makes it worse.
- **Fact**: Talking about your feelings with a good friend can be a helpful first step.

The real question is whether you are temporarily feeling down or sad and the feelings will pass in a few days, or whether you are clinically depressed and need treatment. Actually, one of the main symptoms of clinical depression is that it *does not go away* on its own. When depression goes on for weeks, months, or even longer, it becomes a serious condition—at that point it starts to affect your ability to function in the world.

Because every year millions of Americans struggle with major depression, it has been the subject of thousands of scientific studies, and its symptoms are well-known. Here is what to look for, according to reports from the Nemours Foundation, the National Alliance for the

Mentally Ill, and the National Institute of Health:

- You feel sad or cry a lot, for what may seem like no reason.
- You feel guilty for no reason; you feel like you're no good; you've lost your confidence.
- You can see no point to life, or you feel that nothing good is ever going to happen again.
- You have a negative attitude a lot of the time, or it seems as if you have no feelings at all; you feel numb.
- You do not feel like doing the things you used to like—music, sports, being with friends, going out—and you want people to leave you alone most of the time, including your friends and family.
- You have trouble making decisions. You forget things and find it hard to concentrate.
- You do not care about anything.
- You get irritated often. Little things make you lose your temper; you over-react; you feel anxious.
- You may sleep more than usual, have trouble falling asleep at night, or you wake up really early not get back to sleep.
- You feel aches and pains, but nothing is physically wrong with you.
- Your eating pattern changes: You do not feel like eating, or you eat a lot more. You lose or gain a lot of weight.
- You feel listless and tired most of the time.
- You think about death, or you feel las though you are dying, or you have thoughts about killing yourself.

If you have five or more of these symptoms for more than two weeks, you can assume you are in a major depression. Do not wait and hope that it will go away on its own. Talk to an adult you trust about how you feel. If you can, start with a parent, who will probably be supportive and want to help you feel better.

If you are extremely depressed and are thinking about hurting yourself or considering suicide, get help now. This is a very real medical emergency and an adult must be notified. The same goes if a friend mentions death or suicide to you or shows other warning signs—tell a parent, teacher, or school counselor immediately. Whether for yourself or a friend, going for help is the most important thing a depressed person can do.

IS IT TRUE THAT GAY TEENS ARE MORE AT RISK FOR SUICIDE?

In a word, yes. In fact, SUICIDE is the number one killer of gay teens, according to research carried out beginning in the 1990s by Dr. Gary Remafedi at the University of Minnesota and others. A 1984 report indicated that homosexual and bisexual teens were more than three times more likely to attempt suicide than heterosexual teens. Other research shows that homosexual males are between six and seven times more likely to attempt suicide than their heterosexual counterparts.

From 20 to 35 percent of gay youths try to kill themselves. That is two or three out of every ten gay kids—six times higher than straight teens, according to a study reported in the *Tucson Citizen* in September 2000.

A 1991 University of Minnesota study found that the vast majority of suicide attempts by gay and lesbian adolescents were made within a year before or after they had discovered their sexual orientation. This statistic was reported in *Education Week* in April 2000 in an article titled "Homosexual Students: A Group Particularly Vulnerable to Suicide."

"Adolescence is a difficult time anyway," says Kathleen Neville, a psychotherapist and specialist on gay and lesbian issues, in a March 12, 1998, article in the *Milwaukee Journal Sentinel*. "But when a teen is ashamed of sexual thoughts, feelings or actions and thinks there's nowhere to turn, isolation can contribute to depression and perhaps suicidal thoughts or attempts."

Many gay teenagers are harassed at school and receive no support at home because they are afraid to talk to their parents about their sexual orientation. Even parents who know their teenagers are gay may not know how to give them the help they need. And some parents add to the verbal or physical abuse gay kids get from peers. This combination of abuse and lack of support only adds to a gay teenager's social and emotional isolation and low self-esteem.

This is the biggest risk for gay teenagers: keeping their real feelings bottled up. Also, Neville and other specialists warn that for anyone feeling depressed, gay or not, trying to escape with alcohol or drugs can only make you feel worse and add to your confusion. They suggest that gay teens who feel alone and depressed need to reach out.

- Look to people who will support, not judge you. (Your parents might surprise you.)
- Look for a "gay-friendly organization" by calling a women's shelter or university counseling department in your town for a referral.
- Call the national Gay and Lesbian Hot Line Monday through Friday from 5 to 9 P.M. or Saturday 11 A.M. to 4 P.M. at (888) 843-4564.
- Go to a website for coming out teens—such as OutProud (www.outproud.org) or Youth.org (www.youth.org).
- If there is a gay and lesbian group at your school, join it.

WHY DO A LOT OF TEENAGERS SHOPLIFT?

The most frequent answer from teens who are caught shoplifting? "I don't know." When they do give a reason for their shoplifting, it falls in one of three categories: stress, temptation, and peer pressure (according to the National Retail Security Survey, 1998). Temptation is something everyone can understand—shoplifters give in to it, nonshoplifters do not, at least not this kind of temptation. In the stress category teens whose parents are going through a divorce, for example, might feel that they deserve something good in their life. Or a teen may use stealing as a way of getting back at someone, like a parent or a friend, who has hurt them. Teenage shoplifters might be under obvious pressure from peers or friends ("Hey, we're all lifting something today")

or they might shoplift on their own to prove that they fit in with friends who shoplift. In interviews 66 percent of kids say they hang out with kids who shoplift.

Of these same kids 89 percent say they know other kids who shoplift. Like most teens, you have probably had the experience of going into a store and feeling unwelcome—you may even have been followed around by a clerk who seemed to actually be expecting you to shoplift. You probably resented that treatment—who wouldn't? But here's why it happens: Storeowners know that people between the ages of 13 and 17 account for nearly one-third of all shoplifters arrested.

Most teens are not shoplifters at all. And most teens who shoplift are not professionals—that is, they are not thieves who steal for a living. (The pros usually take expensive items, like clothing and jewelry, that they can easily turn around and sell. Some steal to support a drug habit.) About 70 percent of the time teens and other nonprofessional shoplifters go into a store with no intention of stealing. Many of them steal things they don't really want or need, often for the thrill of what they think of as outsmarting the system. Others steal items that they want but can't afford or aren't allowed to buy—clothes, CDs, cosmetics, cigarettes. Shoplifters are also frequently bored or depressed.

Most nonprofessional shoplifters don't commit other types of crimes. They would never steal anything from your house, for instance.

For many people, including teens, shoplifting is an addiction; it can be just as difficult to stop as drugs or alcohol. In a survey by Shoplifters Alternative 57 percent of adults and 33 percent of juveniles said it was hard for them to stop shoplifting even after getting caught. Drug addicts who are also shoplifting addicts say that "lifting" is as addicting as drugs.

Wonder whether you are at risk? Here are five signs to look for:

- You often think about stealing.
- You think shoplifting doesn't hurt anyone.
- When you are by yourself, you are tempted to shoplift (or you actually do).
- You hang out with people who shoplift.

• You don't think twice about breaking rules, as in cheating on tests or using illegal drugs.

If you have a problem with shoplifting, or you are concerned about a friend, find an adult you trust, and ask them for help with finding shoplifting treatment programs in your community. There are many resources available for teens—hotlines, local hospitals, and community health services groups (check your phone book). Once you or your friend understands and deals with what's triggering the shoplifting habit, you're on your way to overcoming it.

WHAT IS THE REAL CONNECTION BETWEEN SMOKING, DRINKING, AND DEPRESSION?

Teens who smoke or drink will usually tell you it makes them feel better. Drinking or using other drugs, they say, takes the pressure off and helps them forget about dating problems, hassles from their parents, stress at school, or feeling as if they are different from everyone else in the world. Smoking often makes teens feel more in charge of their lives, more like their smoking friends—more grown up.

Sounds pretty good until you look a little deeper.

For instance, teens who smoke face approximately a four-times greater risk of developing depression than nonsmoking teens, according to an October 2000 study reported in the magazine *Pediatrics*. In another study, this one in *Journal of Consulting and Clinical Psychology*, published by the American Psychological Association in April 2001, psychologists studied more than a 1,000 kids (average age 15). They found that the teenagers with high levels of depression (measured by questions that asked how often they felt lonely, or like a failure) were also smoking heavily, which they defined as at least 20 cigarettes a day for six months. They also discovered that the more depressed a teen felt, the more he smoked, and the more he smoked, the more depressed he felt—a vicious circle.

Drinking and depression often go hand in hand, according to the National Institute of Mental Health. They have looked at the findings of many researchers to determine which comes first, and here is their answer: either one, and sometimes you cannot tell which. Sometimes the depression comes first, and people try drinking or drugs as a way to escape it. Other times the alcohol or other drug use comes first, and depression is caused by

• the drug itself, or
• withdrawal from it, or
• the problems that substance use causes.

Those good feelings some teens describe in the early stages of drinking or smoking disappear—sooner or later. With drinking or using other drugs, eventually all you care about is getting high, and once you start it's hard to stop; you need to use more just to feel normal. You may feel good when you're high, but when the beer, wine, hard liquor, or drug wears off, depression sets in.

Furthermore, smoking is as addictive as any drug. In fact, many experts say that the nicotine in tobacco is more addictive than cocaine, heroin, or opium. (Just ask someone who has tried to quit smoking and failed.) One survey of high school students who were daily smokers showed that only 5 percent of them intended to be smoking in five years—but after five years 75 percent of them were still smoking.

Look around you. Most teens are *not* drinking alcohol. Research shows that 70 percent of people between 12 and 20 have not had a drink in the past month, the National Clearinghouse for Alcohol and Drug Information reports.

And two out of three high school students are *not* smoking, although the rate is rising. According to a 1999 national survey by the American Lung Association, 34.8 percent of high schoolers smoke, and 22.4 percent of twelfth graders smoke cigarettes daily. The trouble is lots of these kids think they can quit smoking anytime. But the survey turned up the truth:

Adolescents who smoke regularly can have just as hard a time quitting as long-time smokers. Of adolescents who have smoked at least 100 cigarettes in their lifetime—and that is only five packs of cigarettes—most report that they would like to quit but are not able to. Now *that* is depressing.

WHAT IS THE TRUTH ABOUT TEENS WHO HURT THEMSELVES ON PURPOSE?

Almost all teenagers and other people who deliberately injure themselves are feeling great emotional pain. Self-injury (also called self-mutilation) is the act of deliberately destroying body tissue; and while this may be hard to understand, people sometimes hurt themselves because it makes them feel better. These acts are not one-time things—self-injurers hurt themselves over and over, for months or years.

If you have ever exploded with anger or sobbed because someone you love has died, you know that physical action can sometimes relieve emotional pain. You feel better, even though nothing has really changed. Some people cannot relieve this kind of pain in the usual ways. Why not? Maybe they are not allowed to express emotion in their home. Maybe they have been told always to be strong, never to cry. What they discover is that hurting themselves makes the tension go away, at least for awhile.

Some teens who hurt themselves say that they feel numb and that making themselves feel physical pain lets them know that they are still alive.

About three out of four people who deliberately hurt themselves do it by cutting. (They may use razors, scissors, pins, or even the sharp edge of the tab on a can of soda.) Others burn themselves, hit themselves with objects or their fists until they bruise themselves, pick at scabs and sores to keep them from healing, pull out their hair, or break their bones. Going overboard with body piercing or tattooing also falls in this category. Self-injurious behavior occurs among males and females of any race and at any age, but more girls than boys hurt themselves. Most self-injurers are under 30 and mostself-injury begins in the teen years.

Teens who hurt themselves can be drug and alcohol abusers. Often they have been physically or sexually abused and have kept that a secret. They could also be suffering from an eating disorder.

Although these teens are not trying to hurt themselves permanently, they are at risk each time they injure themselves. Their cuts may need stitches or become infected because the person uses dirty cutting instruments. Sometimes two people who are self-injurers cut themselves and share the cutting instrument—and thus risk spreading HIV and hepatitis. Sores that are not allowed to heal may become severely infected. Nearly all these self-inflicted injuries leave physical scars. Teens who injure themselves on purpose are also more likely to commit suicide later if they don't get help with their underlying problems.

The best thing you can do for a friend who hurts herself is to *be* a friend. It is a disturbing subject to talk about, but you can let your friend know that you don't think she is bad for doing this, and that you care about her and want to help. The next step is to find an adult your friend can trust. Maybe she would feel more able to write about what she is doing in a letter or a journal than to talk directly to the adult. But she needs to communicate with someone who can get her help to stop the behavior and deal with the problems that cause it. Local mental-health hotlines or crisis centers can be a place to start.

Eventually, a professional counselor or therapist will recommend a treatment, which might include a combination of behavioral therapy, an antidepressant medication, and special treatment for any associated problems such as EATING DISORDERS. Some people have found that relieving stress through methods like hypnosis, exercise, or art therapy helps them in their recovery.

Once the problems that cause the hurting behavior begin to be solved, self-injurers find that the urge to harm themselves grows weaker, and their chance for leading healthier, happier lives grows greater.

WHAT IS THE RELATIONSHIP BETWEEN TEEN SUICIDE AND GUNS?

First, a reminder: Suicide is the third leading cause of death for teens, and the rate of suicides among teens is going up.

According to suicide prevention experts, teens with a gun in their home are 30 times more likely to commit suicide than teens without a gun available—and this applies to teens who have no history of mental illness. The risk is greater for those under 16.

The increase in the rate of teen suicide is mainly due to the increase in the rate of suicide by firearms, and the more recent increase in suicide among young African American males is also primarily due to an increase in suicide by firearms. From 1980 to 1992 firearm suicides among 15- to 19-year-olds increased 36 percent, while for preteens ages 10 to 14 the rate climbed a staggering 132 percent. Both increases surpass suicide rate increases by other methods in both age categories.

The risk is greater from handguns than from shotguns; and—as you might guess—if a loaded gun is available, the risk goes up even more.

The Foundation for Suicide Prevention recommends that "guns be removed from homes of all at-risk individuals, and that guns never be stored loaded, as they bestow an increased risk of suicide even to those without evidence of mental illness."

Every 46 minutes a young person kills himself or herself—over 60 percent of the time with a firearm, according to a report in the *New England Journal of Medicine.* Years ago men succeeded in killing themselves more often than women did because they were more apt to use a firearm, the *Journal* reported. But since 1975 firearms account for the highest percentage of completed suicides for women. Now, like men, women most often kill themselves with firearms.

In a survey reported by the Nemours Foundation of 342 students in grades nine through twelve in New York City public high schools, students talked about guns in their homes and about their attitudes toward guns. Almost half the teens surveyed (41 percent) said there had been a gun in their home, and more than half (57%) said that they or a relative had been injured by a gun at some time.

Many people in the United States believe that owning firearms is a constitutional right. Whether or not someone in your home owns a gun, it is the responsibility of adults to protect children and teens from harm by teaching them about gun safety—before anyone gets hurt. When guns are in the home, adults (and teens, if they are responsible for the gun) need to:

- Take the ammunition out of the gun.
- Lock the gun and keep it out of reach of children (39 percent of people who say they own guns do not lock them, and one out of three of them keeps their unlocked guns loaded).
- Lock the ammunition and store it apart from the gun.
- Store the keys for the gun and the ammunition away from the guns and away from other keys, out of reach of children.
- Lock up gun-cleaning supplies (these are often poisonous).

Directory of Services, Organizations, Help Sites, and Hotlines

Services and Organizations

For Volume 2: *Mental Health: Depression, Suicide, and Other Issues*

American Academy of Child and Adolescent Psychiatry
3615 Wisconsin Ave. N.W.
Washington. D.C. 20016-3007
www.aacap.org

American Foundation for Suicide Prevention
120 Wall Street, 22nd Floor
New York, NY 10005
(888) 333-AFSP
www.afsp.org

American Psychiatric Association
1400 K Street N.W.
Washington, D.C. 20005
(888) 357-7924
www.psych.org

American Society of Suicidology
4201 North Connecticut Avenue, Suite 310
Washington, D.C. 20008
(202) 287-2280
www.cyberpage.org/aas.htn

Anxiety Disorders Association of America
11900 Parklawn Drive, Suite 100
Rockville, MD 20852
(301) 231-9350
www.adaa.org

Children and Adults with Attention Deficit Hyperactivity Disorder
8181 Professional Place, Suite 201
Landover, MD 20785
(800) 233-4050
www.chadd.org

Institute for Mental Health Initiatives
Channeling Children's Anger
4545 42nd Street, N.W., Suite 311
Washington, D.C. 20016
(202) 364-7111
www.imhi.org

National Attention Deficit Disorder Association
1788 Second Dtreet, Suite 200
Highland Park, IL 60035
(847) 432-ADDA
www.add.org

National Depressive and Manic Depressive Association
730 N. Franklin Street, Suite 501
Chicago, IL 60610-7204
(800) 826-3632
www.ndmda.org

Suicide Awareness Voices of Education
P.O. Box 24507
Minneapolis, MN 55424-0507
(612) 946-7998
www.save.org

For the Set

American Academy of Family Physicians
11400 Tomahawk Creek Parkway
Leawood, KS 66211-2672
(913) 906-6000
www.aafp.org

American Academy of Pediatrics
141 Northwest Point Boulevard
Elk Grove, IL 60007-1098
(847) 434-4000
www.aap.org

American Medical Association
515 North State Street
Chicago, IL 60610-4377
(312) 464-5000
www.ama-assn.org

American Medical Women's Association
801 North Fairfax Street, Suite 400
Alexandria VA, 22314
(703) 838-0500
www.amwa-doc.org

American Red Cross
431 18th Street, NW
Washington, DC 20006
(202) 639-3400
www.redcross.org

Association for the Care of Children's Health
19 Mantua Road
Mt. Royal, NJ 08061
(609) 224-1742
www.acch.org

Centers for Disease Control and Prevention
1600 Clifton Road
Atlanta, GA 30333
(404) 639-3311
www.cdc.gov

National Center for Health Education
72 Spring Street, Suite 208
New York, NY 10012
(212) 334-9470
www.nche.org

National Health Information Center
Office of Disease Prevention and Health Promotion
P.O. Box 1133
Washington, DC 20013-1133
(800) 336-4797
www.health.gov/nhic

National Institutes of Health
9000 Rockville Pike
Bethesda, MD 20892
(301) 496-4000
www.nih.gov

Office of Alternative Medicine
National Institutes of Health
9000 Rockville Pike
Bethesda, MD 20892
(888) 644-6226
http://nccam.nih.gov

Office of Minority Health Resource Center
P.O. Box 37337
Washington, DC 20013-7337
(800) 444-6472
www.omhrc.gov

U.S. Department of Health and Human Services
200 Independence Avenue, SW
Washington, DC 20201
(877) 696-6775
www.os.dhhs.gov

U.S. Food and Drug Administration
5600 Fishers Lane
Rockville, MD 20857-0001
(888) INFO-FDA
www.fda.gov

World Health Organization
CH-1211
Geneva, Switzerland
www.who.ch

Help Sites and Hotlines

Brain Injury Association
105 North Alfred Street
Alexandria, VA 22314
1-800-444-6443
www.biausa.org

Center for Mental Health Services
5600 Fishers Lane
Rockville, MD 20857
1-800-789-2647
www.mentalhealth.org

National Alliance for the Mentally Ill
200 North Glebe Road, Suite 1015
Arlington, VA 22203-3754
1-800-950-NAMI
www.nami.org

National Hopeline Network
1-800-Suicide
www.suicidehotlines.com

National Institutes of Mental Health
5600 Fishers Lane, Room 7C-02
Bethesda, MD 892-8030
1-800-ANXIETY
1-800-PANIC
www.nimh.nih.gov

National Mental Health Association
1021 Prince Street
Alexandria, VA 22314-2971
1-800-969-NMHA
www.nmha.org

National Mental Health Consumer's Self-Health
  Clearinghouse
1211 Chestnut Street
Philadelphia, PA 10107
1-800-553-4539
www.mhselfhelp.org

Self-Abuse Finally Ends Alternatives Program
7115 West North Avenue, Suite 319
Oak Park, IL 60302
1-800-DON'T CUT
www.selfinjury.com

Suicide Prevention Advocacy Network U.S.A.
5034 Odins Way
Marietta, CA 30068
1-888-649-1366
www.spanusa.org

Glossary

The glossary contains all keywords and their definitions. Keywords that are in capital letters are also entries. The volume(s) in which each keyword appears is indicated in brackets.

A

acupuncture an alternative treatment in which the healthcare provider inserts tiny needles at key places on the patient's body to relieve pain or other symptoms [Vols. 6, 8]

adrenaline hormone that stimulates the heart and other organs to prepare for fighting or fleeing from danger [Vol. 2]

aerobics physical activity that increases the flow of oxygen to the body [Vol. 3]

afterbirth the placenta and associated membranes that are expelled after delivery of an infant [Vol. 3]

agoraphobia a strong and irrational fear of open or public spaces; agoraphobics typically choose to remain in their own homes, only leaving if they can be escorted by someone they trust [Vol. 2]

allergens common everyday substances to which the body's immune system is oversensitive [Vol. 8]

ambient existing or present on all sides [Vol. 6]

amnesia a complete or partial loss of memory [Vol. 2]

ANABOLIC STEROIDS a group of steroids that are similar to the male hormone testosterone, which gives most men larger bodies and bigger skeletal muscles than the typical woman [Vol. 4]

anesthetic drug that produces anesthesia, an insensitivity to pain and other sensations [Vol. 1]

angina chest pains that occur as the result of coronary artery disease, which slows blood flow to the heart muscle [Vol. 4]

ANTIBIOTICS agents that fight bacteria [Vol. 8]

antibodies substances made by the body to attack foreign organisms or chemicals [Vols. 3, 8]

antigens foreign organisms that can provoke an immune response from the body [Vol. 8]

anti-inflammatory an agent that reduces the swelling, pain, redness, and heat usually associated with injury [Vol. 3]

antioxidants a type of phytochemical that seems to prevent cell damage from oxidation, or the loss of electrons, caused by the actions of free radicals; vitamins C and E are antioxidants [Vol. 4]

antiretroviral drug drug used to treat retroviruses, particularly HIV [Vol. 7]

appestat the part of the brain that controls eating behavior [Vol. 4]

appetite suppressants drugs taken to decrease the sense of hunger [Vol. 4]

aquifers underground pools that collect, store, and transfer groundwater [Vol. 6]

arson the deliberate act of starting a fire that destroys property [Vol. 5]

artificial sweeteners chemicals that imitate the sweetness of sugar but have fewer calories; they are used by people who suffer from diabetes mellitus or are trying to lose weight [Vol. 4]

aspartame one of the most popular artificial sweeteners in America; it is found in cereals, soft drinks, gum, yogurt, and low-calorie dessert foods [Vol. 4]

ATHEROSCLEROSIS narrowing of coronary arteries due to a buildup of deposits in them [Vol. 8]

B

bacteria microscopic, one-celled organisms that live both inside and outside the body, some of which can cause disease [Vols. 7, 8]

barrier methods contraceptive methods such as the condom, female condom, and cervical cap or diaphragm that create physical barriers between the sperm and the ovum [Vol. 3]

behavior therapy form of psychotherapy that uses learning and conditioning techniques to change undesirable behavior [Vol. 1]

benign pertaining to noncancerous cells not likely to grow or spread out of control [Vol. 8]

beriberi a disease that occurs when a person does not have enough vitamin B-1, or thiamine, and feels too sick to do anything; the legs become stiff, paralyzed, and painful [Vol. 4]

BIRTH DEFECTS abnormalities present before or after birth [Vol. 3]

blastocyst the embryonic stage at which the fertilized cell implants itself in the uterine wall [Vol. 3]

BLOOD ALCOHOL CONCENTRATION (BAC) the ratio of alcohol volume to blood volume in the body, expressed as a percent [Vols. 1, 5]

blood volume the quantity of blood within the body [Vol. 3]

bone marrow the soft tissue that fills the cavities of most bones, where red blood cells are manufactured [Vol. 3]

C

caesarian the surgical delivery of a baby [Vol. 3]

caffeine a natural stimulant found in the plants used to make tea, coffee, chocolate; an additive found in many foods, including soft drinks and medications [Vol. 4]

capital punishment the legal killing of a person convicted of a crime [Vol. 5]

CARCINOGENS cancer-causing agents [Vol. 8]

carnotite a radioactive mineral that is the source of uranium [Vol. 6]

cell division the means by which cells develop [Vol. 3]

cervix the narrow opening to the uterus [Vol. 3]

CHILD ABUSE physical harm to a child; sexual abuse of a child entails sexual gratification of an adult [Vol. 1]

child neglect failure to provide food, shelter, and medical attention; abandonment is a form of child neglect [Vol. 1]

CHOLESTEROL fatlike substance manufactured by the body and found in certain foods [Vol. 8]

chromosomes threadlike bodies in the nucleus of living cells that carry genes [Vol. 1]

circulatory system the body system through which blood flows [Vol. 3]

CMV retinitis an eye disease caused by cytomegalovirus (CMV) that often occurs in patients with AIDS [Vol. 7]

coma a state of deep, often prolonged unconsciousness, usually the result of injury, disease, or poison, in which a person does not respond to internal or external demands [Vol. 5]

compulsions repeated ritualized behaviors [Vol. 2]

contraception voluntary prevention of pregnancy [Vol. 3]

contraceptive methods chemical, physical, or hormonal methods used to prevent pregancy [Vol. 3]

contractions the pushing action of the uterus during labor [Vol. 3]

controlled substance drugs or other agents that are highly controlled and monitored by the Drug Enforcement Adminstration (DEA) [Vol. 2]

corrosive a substance that gradually weakens or destroys its surroundings such as a chemical that is capable of destroying the metal tank in which it is contained [Vol. 6]

craving intensely urgent need for an addictive substance such as alcohol, tobacco, or illegal drugs [Vol. 1]

crowning the first emergence of the fetus outside the birth canal [Vol. 3]

D

DATE RAPE DRUGS tasteless and odorless drugs that, when added to alcohol, often lead to unconsciousness and difficulty in remembering and that are favored by those who take sexual advantage of others [Vol. 5]

decibel a unit used to measure the relative intensity of sound; abbreviated dB [Vol. 6]

delivery the birthing process [Vol. 3]

delusions false beliefs [Vol. 2]

denial refusing to see a difficult situation as it really is [Vol. 2]

depersonalization uncomfortable feeling of being unreal or detached from one's body or surroundings [Vol. 2]

desertification the spread of an arid environment into areas that were not previously desert [Vol. 6]

detection discovery, usually through testing, of a disease [Vol. 8]

DETOXIFICATION withdrawal of an addictive substance under close medical supervision [Vol. 2]

DIAPHRAGM a muscle in the chest that helps with breathing [Vol. 3]

dietician a person qualified to plan diets for people with special health concerns or for hospitals, schools, or nursing homes [Vol. 4]

dilation and evacuation (D&E) a procedure in which the cervix is opened and the contents of the uterous are removed [Vol. 3]

dilation and extraction (D&X) a procedure in which the cervix is opened and the fetus is removed [Vol. 3]

disenfranchised describes individuals who have little or no power to influence social or political policies that affect them directly [Vol. 5]

disorientation loss of the sense of time or place [Vol. 2]

dissociation mentally separating oneself from a stressful event [Vol. 2]

diuretic substance that increases the volume of urine excreted from the kidneys [Vols. 1, 4]

domestic partner a person who lives with another [Vol. 5]

dopamine chemical in the brain that helps transmit messages between brain cells [Vol. 2]

dysthymia a mild form of depression that lasts for at least two years [Vol. 2]

E

eclampsia a general seizure that may be experienced by a woman after the 24th week of pregnancy [Vol. 3]

effluent waste matter discharged into the environment [Vol. 6]

electroconvulsive therapy treatment in which an electric current is passed through the brain of the anesthetized patient [Vol. 2]

electromagnetic radiation the transfer of energy produced by the motion of electrically charged particles [Vol. 6]

electromagnetic spectrum the range of electromagnetic waves, from the shortest to the longest [Vol. 6]

emission something that is released or discharged [Vol. 6]

endometrium the outer lining of the uterine wall [Vol. 3]

endorphins and enkephalins natural substances produced by the brain to reduce pain; these chemicals are also released during strenuous exercise, such as marathon racing [Vol. 4]

endurance the ability of the body to withstand physical stress or repetition [Vol. 4]

euphoria an exaggerated feeling of well-being that has no basis in reality [Vol. 1]

euthanasia enabling or assisting a person with terminal or painful illness to die [Vol. 5]

F

fertile able to conceive [Vol. 3]

fetal death the death of a fetus after week 28 of a pregnancy [Vol. 3]

flashback unexpected recurrence of the effects of a hallucinogenic drug long after its original use [Vol. 1]

foreskin a retractable fold of skin over the head of the penis [Vol. 3]

free radicals molecules having at least one unpaired electron that appear to cause certain diseases and to be involved in the aging process [Vol. 4]

frequency the number of waves that pass a certain point during one second [Vol. 6]

fructose sugar found in fruits, saps, and some vegetables [Vol. 4]

fungi plantlike organisms, including molds and mushrooms; some fungi can cause infections [Vol. 8]

G

genes the part of living cells that carries specific characteristics and passes them on from one generation to the next [Vol. 1, 7]

gestation the time a fetus spends developing in the uterous, from conception to birth [Vol. 3]

glucose a sugar that is the main fuel for body cells [Vol. 8]

goiter a condition in which the thyroid gland becomes swollen; one cause is too little iodine in the diet [Vol. 4]

glycogen a starch stored in the muscles that can be converted into glucose for energy [Vol. 4]

graffiti markings, initials, and sketches on walls, fences, and sidewalks, often used by gangs to mark territories [Vol. 5]

H

HALLUCINATIONS false perceptions [Vol. 2]

hate speech public communication that expresses the speaker's hatred, disapproval, or prejudice against certain groups of people [Vol. 5]

HEART ATTACK damage or even death to a part of the heart muscle that occurs when blood flow to the area is stopped because of a blood clot or coronary artery disease [Vols. 4, 8]

hernia a protrusion of an organ or tissue through an opening in its surrounding walls especially in the abdominal region of the body [Vol. 1]

heterosexism prejudice or discrimination against homosexuals [Vol. 5]

highly active antiretroviral therapy (HAART) a combination of several—usually three—antiretroviral drugs used to treat HIV and AIDS; often called an "AIDS cocktail" [Vol. 7]

homeopathy treatment of a disease in which small doses of a remedy that in a healthy person would produce symptoms of the disease being treated [Vols. 6, 8]

HORMONES chemical substances produced by glands that affect the functions of body organs and tissues [Vols. 1, 4]

hydrocarbons compounds containing carbon and hydrogen [Vol. 6]

hymen a thin membrane that partly covers the vagina, which may be torn by sexual intercourse [Vol. 3]

hyperbaric treatment placing a serverely burned patient in a chamber in which air pressure is raised to expose burns to high levels of oxygen for faster healing [Vol. 5]

I

implantation the positioning of a blastocyst in the uterine wall [Vol. 3]

INSULIN a hormone that enables cells to absorb glucose [Vol. 8]

irritable bowel syndrome (IBS) a condition in which irregular muscular movements in the small intestine and colon cause constipation, gas, bloating, and severe pain [Vol. 4]

J

jaundice a disease caused by an accumulation of bodily waste products in the blood when liver function is impaired, which causes the skin and eyes to turn yellow [Vol. 7]

juveniles persons under the age of 18 [Vol. 5]

L

lactose sugar found in milk and other dairy products [Vol. 4]

lactose intolerance a condition in which the small intestine fails to produce the enzyme, lactase, which is needed to break down milk, sugar, or lactose; the result is gas, bloating, and diarrhea [Vol. 4]

laparoscopy surgical inspection of the abdominal cavity and pelvis through a lit tube [Vol. 3]

LIFE EXPECTANCY the number of years a person is expected to live [Vol. 5]

life support artificial means of sustaining life [Vol. 5]

ligaments bands of tough tissue that tie bones to one another to form joints [Vol. 4]

lymphocyte a type of white blood cell that helps the immune system fight off infection and disease [Vol. 7]

M

macrophage a large white blood cell that surrounds and destroys microbes and is part of the immune system [Vol. 7]

malignant pertaining to cancerous cells that are likely to spread uncontrollably and to damage tissues of the body; cancerous [Vol. 8]

malnutrition condition of poor or unhealthy nutrition brought on by an inadequate or unbalanced diet [Vol. 1]

metabolize break down chemically within the body [Vol. 1]

METASTASIS process of malignant tumor cells spreading beyond their starting point in the body [Vol. 8]

microbe germ [Vol. 7]

microbicides agents that kill viruses and bacteria [Vol. 7]

microorganisms extremely small organisms, primarily bacteria, fungi, protozoa, and viruses [Vol. 6]

mill tailings the waste removed from an underground mine, which includes small particles of mine waste as well as rocks and other unmarketable materials [Vol. 6]

MORTALITY death [Vol. 5]

mutation unregulated changes in cells [Vol. 8]

mutual masturbation sexual stimulation in which two people bring each other to orgasm, either at the same time or one after the other, without intercourse [Vol. 7]

N

naturopathy treatment of a disease that emphasizes the use of natural agents such as heat, cold, water, sunshine, and physical therapies [Vols. 6, 8]

negotiation process in which differences are worked out and a solution is reached [Vol. 5]

neurotransmitter a substance that carries signals from one nerve cell to another [Vol. 2]

neutrophil a large white blood cell containing small sacs filled with enzymes that digest and destroy microbes and is part of the immune system [Vol. 7]

nicotine a toxic and highly addictive drug found in tobacco [Vol. 1]

nitrates additives used in cured meats to protect against food poisoning; has been linked to the production of possible cancer-causing agents in the human stomach [Vol. 4]

nomadic roaming from place to place [Vol. 6]

Nonoxynol-9 the active ingredient in spermicides available in the United States, which kills the sperm or inhibits its movement [Vol. 3]

norephinephrine a hormone and a neurotransmitter that causes heart rate, blood pressure, and blood sugar levels to increase and the blood vessels to constrict, preparing the body to meet stressful challenges [Vol. 2]

nuclei the plural of *nucleus;* the positively charged center of an atom [Vol. 6]

nutrient a substance found in foods, drinks, or diet supplements that the body needs to be able to grow, heal from injuries and illnesses, and perform daily functions; the six major nutrients are carbohydrates, fats, proteins, water, vitamins, and minerals [Vol. 4]

nutritionist a person who studies how food affects health and well-being [Vol. 4]

O

obsessions recurring disturbing thoughts or mental images [Vol. 2]

opportunistic infections rare infections that occur in people with weakened immune systems [Vol. 7]

ORGASM the peak or climax of sexual stimulation; in men, the ejaculation of semen from the penis; in women, the rhythmic contraction of the muscles around the vagina [Vol. 7]

ostracized excluded from participation [Vol. 5]

overuse injury an injury caused by repetitive motion [Vol. 4]

ovulation the release of an ovum from the ovary [Vol. 3]

oxytocin the hormone that makes labor start [Vol. 3]

P

panic attack sudden feeling of terror accompanied by physical sensations of extreme fear [Vol. 2]

paralysis the inability to move muscles, such as those in the legs and arms [Vol. 5]

paranoia irrational belief that others are out to harm you, a feature of some mental illnesses [Vols. 1, 2, 5]

paraplegic person who is paralyzed from the waist down [Vol. 5]

parasite organism that lives in or on another organism called a host; parasites depend on hosts for all of their nourishment [Vols. 7, 8]

parasitosis hallucination that many insects are crawling over or under the skin [Vol. 1]

parole the release of a convicted criminal from prison under strict conditions [Vol. 5]

particulates very small, separate particles; can be liquid droplets or tiny solid particles [Vol. 6]

passive smoking breathing in secondhand smoke, or smoke that is generated by another person [Vol. 1]

pathogens organisms that cause disease [Vol. 8]

PEER PRESSURE influence exerted on a person by their friends and other contemporaries [Vol. 5]

pellagra a disease that involves weakness, lack of appetite, diarrhea, and indigestion; it develops from not having enough vitamin B-3 or niacin and the amino acid tryptophan in the diet [Vol. 4]

perineum the area surrounding the genital and excretory organs [Vol. 3]

phytochemicals substances found in some plant foods such as fresh fruits and vegetables that seem to help prevent diseases [Vol. 4]

pitchblende a brownish-black mineral that contains large amounts of uraninite [Vol. 6]

plateau the point in a weight-loss program at which a person finds it difficult to lose any more weight [Vol. 4]

point source pollutants contaminants from a known source such as a drainage pipe [Vol. 6]

premature labor labor that occurs before the fetus is fully developed and ready to be born and survive on its own, usually defined as before week 38 of pregnancy [Vol. 3]

productivity ability to get things done and produce results; the rate of production [Vol. 6]

primary standards standards set by the Clean Air Act to protect public health [Vol. 6]

psychoactive capable of causing dramatic mood changes [Vol. 1]

purging trying to counteract overeating by vomiting, using laxatives, enemas, diuretics, or excessive exercise or dieting [Vol. 4]

R

racism prejudice or discrimination based on race or ethnicity [Vol. 5]

relapse a return to using an addictive substance after attempting to give it up [Vol. 1]

repression the burying of a painful memory or emotion [Vol. 2]

resistance the ability of a body to develop immunity to certain foods, drugs, toxins, diseases, or other stimuli [Vol. 7]

resuscitated brought back to life by forcing the heart to pump and blowing air into the lungs; also called cardiopulmonary resuscitation, or CPR [Vol. 3]

RETROVIRUS virus that infects cells by inserting its RNA into them, instead of DNA as most viruses do [Vol. 7]

R.I.C.E the usual treatment for sprains: rest, ice, compress, and elevate [Vol. 4]

rickets childhood bone disease often caused by a lack of calcium, phosphate, or vitamin D; the bones become soft, bent, bumpy, and abnormally shaped [Vol. 4]

risk factors factors that increase someone's chances of getting a disease but do not necessarily cause it [Vol. 8]

rush a sudden feeling of intense euphoria brought on by the use of certain drugs [Vol. 1]

S

safe houses places where victims of domestic abuse can live temporarily free of abuse and harassment [Vol. 5]

satiety the sense of fullness that comes at the end of a meal [Vol. 4]

secondary standards set by the Clean Air Act to protect public welfare [Vol. 6]

SELF-HELP GROUPS collections of people with similar problems or in similar situations who come together for aid and support [Vol. 5]

serotonin a hormone and a neurotransmitter that helps transmit messages between cells, stimulate smooth muscles, and regulate learning, sleep, and mood; found in the brain, blood, serum, and the mucous membrane of the stomach [Vol. 2]

sexism prejucice or discrimination based on sex [Vols. 3, 5]

side-stream smoke the smoke that a nonsmoker inhales from the environment [Vol. 1]

sludge in sewage treatment, thick, solid matter that has settled out of wastewater in tanks or basins [Vol. 6]

SOBRIETY CHECKPOINTS roadblocks set up to stop, identify, and arrest those who are driving while intoxicated [Vol. 5]

social norms behaviors generally expected and accepted by society [Vol. 5]

social pressures influences in society to think, choose, or act in certain ways [Vol. 5]

socioeconomic status the position a person or group has in society based on family background, education, and income [Vol. 5]

speculum a long, hollow, lighted device used to view the inside of the vagina and cervix [Vol. 3]

stalking following or pursuing another person in a menacing way or with apparent intent to injure them [Vol. 5]

starch complex carbohydrates found in foods such as breads, cereals, pastas, and rice; some vegetables, especially corn and potatoes, also contain a lot of starch; during digestion starches are broken down into simple sugars, which are used as a fuel for body activities [Vol. 4]

sterile unable to produce or support life; unproductive [Vol. 6]

stillbirth a baby that is born dead [Vol. 3]

substance abuse excessive use of alcohol, drugs, tobacco, or other addictive substances [Vol. 1]

sucrose table sugar; processed from sugarcane and sugar beet plants and used as a sweetener [Vol. 4]

sulfites preservatives found in a range of products, including potato chips, bottled juices, and canned fruits, vegetables, and soups; can cause allergic reactions, including asthma attacks [Vol. 4]

T

tendon a band or cord of tissue that connects a muscle to a bone [Vol. 4]

teratogens substances such as cigarette smoke, alcohol, and some drugs, which are known to cause birth defects [Vols. 1, 3]

tinnitus a constant ringing in the ears caused by damage to the auditory nerve [Vol. 6]

TOLERANCE capacity of the body to endure or become less responsive to a substance with repeated use [Vols. 1, 2]

transfusion the transfer of one person's blood into another person's body [Vol. 7]

transuranic wastes wastes created from the production of nuclear fuel and weapons, such as protective clothing, equipment, tools, and contaminated soils [Vol. 6]

tremors trembling or shaking [Vol. 2]

TUMOR mass of cells produced as a result of uncontrolled cellular growth [Vol. 8]

U

urethra tube that drains urine from the bladder to the outside of the body [Vol. 3]

uterine lining the buildup of blood and nutrients on the inside wall of the uterus that supports and protects the developing fetus [Vol. 3]

V

vegan a type of vegetarian who only eats plant-derived foods, excluding even animal by-products, such as eggs, milk, and butter [Vol. 6]

VIRUSES infectious microorganisms that can enter the body, target particular types of tissues, and damage cells [Vols. 7, 8]

volatile organic compounds substances that react with sunlight to form new pollutant compounds [Vol. 6]

Z

zygote a fertilized ovum [Vol. 3]

Further Reading and Internet Sites

For Volume 2: Mental Health, Depression and Suicide

Altman, Linda Jacobs. *Plague and Pestilence: A History of Infectious Disease.* Berkeley Heights, NJ: Enslow Publishers, Inc., 1998.

American Diabetes Association. *American Diabetes Association Complete Guide to Diabetes.* New York: Bantam Books, 2000.

Benowitz, Steven I. *Cancer.* Berkeley Heights, NJ: Enslow Publishers, Inc., 1999.

Cameron, Heather. *Different but the Same: Young People Talk about Living with Serious Illness.* Melbourne: Lothian Publishing Company, 1999.

Carmichael, Cynthia G. *AIDS and HIV Essentials.* Pompano, FLA: Health Studies Institute, 1999.

Centers for Disease Control and Prevention. *Preventing Emerging Infectious Diseases: A Strategy for the 21st Century.* Atlanta, GA: CDC, 1998.

Dahm, Nancy Hassett. *Mind, Body, and Soul: A Guide to Living with Cancer.* Garden City, NJ: Taylor Hill Publishing, 2001.

Diamond, John W. *An Alternative Medicine Definitive Guide to Cancer.* Puyallop, WA: Future Medicine Publishing, 1997.

Giblin, James Cross. *When Plague Strikes: The Black Death, Smallpox, and AIDS.* New York: Harper Collins, 1997.

Latta, Sara L. *Food Poisoning and Foodborne Diseases.* Berkeley Heights, CA: Enslow Publisher, Inc. 1999.

MacIejko, James J. *The ABC's of Coronary Heart Disease.* Chelsea, MI: Sleeping Bear Press, 2001.

Pinsky, Laura, and Paul Harding Douglas. *The Essential AIDS Fact Book.* New York: Simon & Schuster, 1996.

Piver, Steven M., and Gene Wilder. *Gilda's Disease: Personal Experiences and Authoritative Medical Advice on Ovarian Cancer.* New York: Bantam Doubleday, 1998.

Schoeberlein, Deborah. *Every Body: Preventing HIV and Other Sexually Transmitted Diseases among Young Teens.* Carbondale: RAD Educational Programs, 2000.

Yount, Lisa. *Epidemics.* San Diego: Lucent, 2000.

www.infoweb.org [HIV Info Web]
Offers a host of information on HIV-related topics, including news of treatments, alternative medicine, and prevention.

www.iwannaknow.org [I Wanna Know]
Provides teens with straight talk about STDs, including descriptions of the diseases and how to prevent them; features a teen chat room, games, and ways to test knowledge about STDs.

www.leukemia.org [Leukemia and Lymphoma Society]
Provides news and information regarding the Leukemia and Lymphoma Society and ways to improve the quality of life for patients and families.

www.cancernet.nci.nih.gov [The National Cancer Institute's Cancer Net]
Publishes current information from the National Cancer Institute on types of cancer, cancer treatments, genetics, risk factors, prevention, and more.

http://cancer.med.upenn.edu [University of Pennsylvania Cancer Center]
Provides information on cancer types, treatments, and research news from introductory to in-depth levels.

www.tchin.org [Congenital Heart Disease Information and Resources]
Offers access to a "teen lounge" for children with heart disease and includes book reviews, support groups, and a resource room.

For the Set

American Academy of Family Physicians. *Family Health and Medical Guide.* Dallas: Word Publishing, 1996.

American College of Physicians. *American College of Physicians Complete Home Medical Guide.* New York: DK Publishing, 1999.

American Medical Association. *American Medical Association Family Medical Guide.* New York: Random House, 1994.

American Medical Women's Association. *The Women's Complete Healthbook.* New York: Dell Publishing Company, Inc., 1997.

Anderson, Kenneth N., ed. *Mosby's Medical Dictionary.* St. Louis: Mosby, 1994.

Barrett, Stephen, et al. *Consumer Health.* New York: McGraw-Hill, 1997.

Berkow, Robert, and Mark H. Beers, eds. *The Merck Manual of Medical Information: Home Edition.* Whitehouse Station, NJ: Merck Research Laboratories, 2000.

Caravella, Philip. *The Art of Being a Patient: Taming Medicine: An Insider's Guide: Become a Proactive Partner and Self-Advocate of Your Own Health by Understanding.* Bloomington, IN: 1st Books Library, 2000.

Columbia University College of Physicians and Surgeons. *The Columbia University College of Physicians and Surgeons Complete Home Medical Guide.* New York: Crown, 1995.

Columbia University's Health Education Program. *The Go Ask Alice Book of Answers: A Guide to Good Physical, Sexual, and Emotional Health.* New York: Henry Holt, 1998.

Eniola, Anthony. *ABCs of Healthy Living.* Hallandale, FL: Aglob Publishing, 2001.

Faber, Adele, and Elaine Mazlish. *How to Talk So Kids Will Listen & How to Listen So Kids Will Talk.* Mamaroneck, NY: International Center for Creative Thinking, 1990.

Harvard Medical School. *Harvard Medical School Family Health Guide.* New York: Simon & Schuster, 1999.

Mayo Clinic. *Mayo Clinic Family Health Book: The Ultimate Home Reference.* New York: William Morrow, 1998.

Tipley, Donald F., Thomas Q. Morris, and Lewis P. Rowland. *The Columbia University College of Physicians and Surgeons Complete Home Medical Guide.* New York: Crown, 1985.

www.healthatoz.com [Health A to Z: Your Family Health Site]
Offers interactive tools for setting up a personal health calendar, homepage, prescription reminders, and subscriptions to health news; offers opportunities to e-mail healthcare professionals and chat with users.

www.healthfinder.com [Healthfinder]
Gives teens advice on prevention, self-care, and quality care; offers access to health-related library services, news, and professional research; run by the U.S. Department of Health and Human Services.

www.mayoclinic.com [Mayo Clinic]
Offers interactive tools to help you "take charge of your health," including a personal health scorecard, healthy lifestyle planners, and decision guides; provides information on health topics and answers to frequently asked questions from Mayo specialists.

www.medicinenet.com [Medicine Net]
Provides consumer medical information from U.S. board-certified physicians, including guides to over-the-counter and prescription drugs.

www.reutershealth.com [Reuters Health]
Features links to consumer, industry, and professional health news.

www.nlm.nih.gov [United States National Library of Medicine]
Provides online catalog access to the world's largest medical library; features three databases: Medline Plus answers health questions, Medline/PubMed summarizes articles from medical journals, and Clinical Trials let you know about research studies.

Set Index

Bold numbers refer to volume numbers and page numbers of main entries. Page numbers in regular type indicate other mentions of entries and terms. *Italic* numbers and letters refer to charts *(c)*, marginal features *(f)*, illustrations *(i)*, and tables *(t)*.

poliomyelitis, 8:127
pollutant standards index (PSI), 6:66–67, 66c
pollution
    agricultural, 6:67–68
    air, 6:16–17, 17t, 29i
    chemical, 6:29–32
    noise, 6:57–58, 57f, 98–99
    non-point source, 6:34, 87
    point source, 6:85, 87
    soil and land, 6:68–69
    thermal, 6:79–80
    water, 6:87–88, 91–92
polychlorinated biphenyls (PCBs), 6:69
polygamy, 3:93
pornography, 3:93
postpartum blues, 2:76f, 3:93
postpartum depression, 2:76–77, 76f, 3:94
posttraumatic-stress disorder (PTSD), 2:77, 112–113
preeclampsia, 3:65
pregnancy, 3:94–97, 95f, 96c
    exercise, 3:49–50, 50f, 4:56
    first trimester, 3:97–98
    herbs and, 3:61–64, 62–63t
    high blood pressure during, 3:65
    HIV transmission during, 8:23
    prevention of, 3:20, 30, 47, 51f, 98–102, 101t, 142
    risks of, 3:145
    second trimester, 3:102–103, 103i
    third trimester, 3:103–104
    tobacco, alcohol, and drug use and, 1:122–123, 122c, 3:24–25
    unintended. See unintended pregnancy
    weight and, 4:101–102
premature labor, 3:43
prenatal care, 3:104–105, 4:101–102
prenatal development, 3:105–107
prenuptial agreement, 3:75f
prepared childbirth, 3:107–108

prescription drugs:
    addiction and, 1:21–23, 158
    drug overdose and, 1:164–165
    illegal use of, 1:171
preservatives in foods, 4:102–103
prisons. See jails
probation, 5:89
processed foods, 4:103–104
productivity and noise pollution, 6:57
product recalls, 5:95f
progestins, 3:108
prophylaxis, 7:79
prostate cancer, 8:127–128
protective clothing. See safety equipment
proteins, 4:104–105
psychiatrist, 2:79
psychoactive, 1:120f
psychoactive drugs, 1:123–124
psychologist, 2:79
psychosis, 1:124, 2:79–80
psychotherapy, 2:80–82, 81f
PTSD (posttraumatic-stress disorder), 2:77, 112–113
puberty, 3:108–109, 145–146
public-transportation injuries, 5:90
pulmonary disease, chronic obstructive (COPD), 8:60, 60t
pulse, 4:105
purging, 4:38
pyramids, food, 4:64–66, 65i, 121i

Q

quackery, 8:128. See also alternative medicine

R

R.I.C.E., 4:54
rabies, 8:128–129
radiation, 6:58–59, 69–70, 69f
radiation therapy, 8:47–48
radioactive processed foods. See food, irradiated
radon gas, 6:13, 44, 71–72, 92

range of motion. See exercise, flexibility and
rape, 3:125–126, 5:90–91. See also sexual assault and rape
rape crisis centers, 5:91–92
raves, 1:124–125
RDA for pregnant women, 3:84t
recalls of products, 5:95f
recreational and leisure injuries, 5:92–93
recycling, 6:72–74
    conservation and, 6:34, 100
    process of, 6:73–74, 74i
    rates by product, 6:73c
    uses for products, 6:72–73
relapse, 1:20
relaxation therapy, 2:82–85
repetitive-motion injuries, 5:93–94, 94f
reporting and tracking HIV/AIDS, 7:60–61
reporting and tracking STDs, 7:72–73, 92–93
repression, 2:39
reproductive organs:
    female, 3:110–111
    male, 3:111
reproductive technologies, 3:112
resistance, 7:50
respiratory diseases and tobacco use, 1:141–142
resuscitation, 3:43f
retinal detachment, 8:84t
retrovirus, 7:80
ReVia, 1:115
Reye's syndrome, 8:129
rheumatic heart disease, 8:129–130
rheumatoid arthritis, 8:31–32
Rh factor, 3:104f
rhythm method, 3:112
rickets, 4:80
Ritalin, 2:33f
road rage, 5:94
Rocky Mountain spotted fever, 8:130
Roe v. Wade. See abortion, laws concerning
Rohypnol, 1:71
roller-blade injuries, 5:75
RU-486. See abortion
rubella, 8:130
running. See jogging
rush, 1:41, 113

S

SAD. See seasonal affective disorder
Safe Drinking Water Act, 6:46–47, 86, 88
safe houses, 5:68f
safer sex, 3:112–113, 7:80–82
safety belts, 5:94–95, 94f
safety equipment, 5:95, 95f
safety rules, general, 5:95–96
Salmonella, 8:131–132
same-sex relationships, 3:113–115, 148. See also homosexuality
sarcoma, 8:132
satiety, 4:34
saturated fats, 4:106
scabies, 7:82
scarlet fever, 8:132
schizophrenia, 2:85–87, 85f, 86i, 111–112
school sports, 4:106–107
school violence, 5:80f, 96–99, 98t. See also violence, mental health and
scoliosis, 8:132
scooters and injuries, 5:93f
screening, genetic, 8:87f
screening, health, adult, 8:91, 91t
scurvy, 4:107
seasonal affective disorder (SAD), 2:87, 113–114
seat belts, 5:94–95, 94f
secondhand smoke, 1:125, 141
self-help groups, 5:42, 101. See also support groups
self-injury, 2:123
semen, 3:115
septic systems, 6:74–75
serotonin, 2:29, 32, 41
serving size, 4:107–108, 108t
set point, 4:108–109
sewage, 6:75–76
sex. See sexual intercourse
sex, alcohol, and drugs, 1:41–42, 3:115–116, 115f, 7:25–26
sex during and after pregnancy, 3:116–117
sex organs:
    female, 3:110–111
    male, 3:111
sexual abuse. See dating abuse; incest; sexual assault and rape